EVERYBODY
NEEDS
SOMEBODY

EVERYBODY NEEDS SOMEBODY

REDISCOVER THE VALUE OF RELATIONSHIPS
MAKE RELATIONSHIPS WORK FOR YOU
BECOME A FULFILLED AND BETTER PERSON

MUSA BAKO

authorHOUSE®

AuthorHouse™ UK Ltd.
1663 Liberty Drive
Bloomington, IN 47403   USA
www.authorhouse.co.uk
Phone: 0800.197.4150

Published by AuthorHouse 02/19/2014

ISBN: 978-1-4918-7516-2 (sc)
ISBN: 978-1-4918-9615-0 (hc)
ISBN: 978-1-4918-7517-9 (e)

DEDICATION

To my beautiful and adorable wife, Eunice Meque Bako.

You surpass all women.
You are the best gift ever.

An innovative, resourceful, industrious, inspirational, kind, and generous woman you are. Meeting you, knowing you, loving you, and being married to you is a beautiful and exciting adventure and has been very fruitful.

You are a great part of who, what, and where I am today.
Thank you for everything you continue to do.

Love you loads, my sweetheart.

CONTENTS

ACKNOWLEDGEMENTS

I am thankful to the Almighty God for His sufficient grace and the inspiration to write. I am grateful for the leadership and ministry of my father in the Lord and the General Overseer of The Redeemed Christian Church of God (RCCG), Pastor Enoch A. Adeboye, and his wife, our Mummy, Pastor Folu Adeboye. Thanks, Coach, for your rich input in my life. I am grateful to the leadership of members of the RCCG UK Executive Council, Pastor Agu Irikwu, Pastor Kola Bamgbade, Pastor Andrew Adeleke, and my province pastor, Janet Adedipe. Thank you for the roles you play in my life. I would also like to say a big thank you to Tamara Ng'ambi and Sarah Akpaka, who continue to support me in proofreading my script; you two are gifts and very special to me, thank you. Thank you to Dorcas Rheece, Melissa Rangmen, and Jethro Men, my lovely children, for their continued understanding. I love you loads. Finally, I am grateful to all RCCG Victory Assembly members for your prayers and support. I am proud of you all.

PREFACE

The best gift that we all have is the people in our lives. The people in our lives are worth more than all the silver and gold in the world. They are worth more than career success, business breakthroughs, and all the wealth this world can ever give. We all need people; we all need people to enjoy the beauty of God's creation. We all need people to share our life stories, our adventures, and the beautiful experiences that life affords us. We all need people to share our lives with; life would be empty without them. You can have all the success in the world, rise to the top, and have enough money, but with no people to share your life with, life loses its meaning. It becomes empty, boring, and depressing. True success, actually, is not to be measured by worldly goods and material acquisitions but by the quality of relationships you enjoy. In Africa, where I come from, wealth is not seen in the light of what you have but the people in your life.

The God of all creation Himself looked at Adam, the first man, at the beginning of creation and said, "It is not good that the man should be alone" (**Genesis 2:18**). Ecclesiastes 4:9 says, "Two are better than one." You can never be better off, happier, inspired, or fulfilled just by yourself. I have made a great deal of progress since my wife Eunice came into my life; together we have inspired, motivated, and empowered each other in our various endeavours. I can also say by experience that I am where I am today because of the various people God surrounded me with. I first met Eunice in 1986 through her cousin. I came to work with the Redeemed Christian Church of God (RCCG) in 1993 after a friend introduced me to the mission. In 1997, I was recommended for a foreign mission and went to pastor a church in Germany. We met a beautiful lady at the RCCG Headquarters and came to know and love her very much; she played a significant role in our journey to the UK in February of 2000. In some way, the many people I met on the way have made significant contributions to making me who I am today. Everybody really needs somebody.

Relationships are really beautiful; they make the world alive and exciting to live in. When you are alone and by yourself, life becomes empty, boring, and depressing. All people are a gift from God, whether they are white, black, yellow, or brown. God brings people into our lives because we are created to be connected and dependent on each other. No one person is entirely sufficient, having everything and needing nothing whatsoever from another person. No man can survive all by himself without input from others. There is always something that a person may never have, a height that he may never reach, or a success he may never achieve until somebody comes into his life and makes a little contribution. Our stories and our destinies are all interconnected.

We all have come to this world for a reason. Every individual on earth is born gifted and equipped. We all have come to this world blessed, having an inherent ability to succeed in what we were born for. But the gifts and the abilities we carry inside us are brought alive and released into use as we form and mature in our relationships. We all can make a difference in somebody's life. We all have something to contribute to our world. This world and the people in it exist for a purpose; people don't exist accidentally, irrespective of how or where they were born. We all come by design, according to God's good purpose.

Many times, when people are connected, it is destiny that brought them together; this is so because they each have something to contribute. This is why you should never undermine anybody. Never take anybody for granted. Never abuse a relationship you have with somebody. Do all you can to draw people into your life and keep them. We all need to discover the value of people, recognise their roles, be aware of the contribution they bring, understand how the relationship works, know how to keep people in our lives, and know how to bring out the best in them. You can be the most intelligent and gifted person on earth, but without the right people in your life, you are not going to achieve your potential.

There is something good in everybody

Yes, there is something good in everybody; everybody has something to offer the world, and everybody can be a blessing. No human being exists by himself; God made us all. There is no one person who came about as an accident, regardless of the circumstances in which they were conceived. Everything God has ever made has value, is beautiful, and has a purpose. There is nothing that God made that lacks value or is without purpose. You have value, you have a purpose, and you are born for an assignment here on earth.

There is something significant about you. You are here on earth for something very important: the reason you were created. As such, in your journey through life, you have got to establish what that is and make a decision to bring out the good that is in you to touch humanity. God did not make you empty, neither did He make you devoid of resources; inherent in you is everything you need to fulfil your purpose, waiting to be released. You are a creative being embedded with special abilities. You are empowered from the womb to become great in life. You can achieve great things, you can climb to the height of your dreams, and you can reach that goal you set for yourself. You are a blessing and a miracle to your generation, you are one of a kind, and there is no other person like you. Perhaps you do not feel like it, perhaps your journey thus far has been rough and filled with blunders and failures. I can understand that life can be full of ups and downs. We all experience challenges. From time to time, we all face tough and difficult situations, but whatever comes your way, and whatever you have been through, does not have any power over your destiny, unless you allow it to dominate your resolve.

Whatever you have been through in life cannot change the fact that you are born to achieve something specific here on earth; you have been created to be a blessing to your generation. You may not always feel like it, but there is a treasure lying on the inside of you, waiting to be discovered and released. As you are reading this book, I sense something about you is about to shift; I sense the Spirit of God will create a new thing in you, and as a result, generations after you will tell your story. Your destiny is unfolding right now; where you are heading is greater than where you are coming from. God planned your life that way. In your journey to the future, you are going to come in contact with all kinds of people; they are part of the story, your story. Some of the people you are going to meet will be your introducers, helping you to find your place and introducing you to people. Some of these people will be your ladder to the next level of your journey; some will become your challenges to provoke you to develop yourself and bring out the best in you. Some will be your friends and covenant partners. You will need them when you are starting to tire; they will help rekindle the fire in you.

Everybody you come in contact with is key to your next level; everybody God brings your way is relevant in some fashion. It does not matter what form your experience with them takes. God does not bring people together just for the sake of it; everybody you come in contact with has something to do with your destiny, and there is a role they all play in that. You need to know how everybody fits in; you need to develop relationships where you can and allow God to have His way. Every relationship counts, everybody is relevant, every relationship can have a significant impact on you. We all need people. You need people, and God will bring them your way. You need to know how to walk with people, because you need them; no one can succeed in anything alone. And never forget that there are things in life you may never have, until somebody comes into your life and gives them to you. There are places you may never go until somebody comes into your life and takes you there. There are things you may never know until you meet somebody and he shows you. Also there are people who are crucial in your life; you need them to reach a certain height in life. However, you may never meet such people until somebody comes into your life and introduces you to them. We all need certain people to become the best that we ought to be; our destiny is tied to people. That is why God said it is not good for man to be alone. You need to value people and learn how to keep them in your life.

If you don't know how to keep people, you lose them. When you lose the people you need, you interrupt the flow of help and make room for a cycle to form in your journey to destiny, which will hinder your progress. You don't have to go round in a cycle; break it today by learning to keep the precious people God brought into your life. A lot of people separate not because they are not meant to be together or meant for each other but because they offend and hurt each other. We all have the tendency to hurt people; I have seen that happen even between the best of friends, between man and wife, between two good people and genuine lovers. We all need to learn how to deal with hurts. If you don't know how to deal with hurts, you are going to walk away from the people who really matter in your destiny and destroy what is of value to you.

The power of forgiveness is what can subdue offences and heal all hurts. People separate and end relationships not only because they hurt each other (hurts are common to man; everybody makes blunders from time to time), but also because very few people know the power of forgiveness. Without forgiveness, many have walked away from what was once precious to them, have divorced, have closed down companies they started, have quit doing what they enjoyed doing. Others have abandoned what makes them come alive, while some have chosen to walk away from a place, church, or community they were connected to in order to break away. Some have killed, maimed, and betrayed people they once loved because they could not forgive.

Ultimately, what we end up becoming in life, the contribution we make to our world and the impact we have on people's lives, will depend on our choices. It is good to be surrounded by good people, but choose to be a good person yourself. It is good to have good friends, but you must choose to be a good friend yourself. It is good to have people you care about and want to support you, but you should care and be supportive too. What really counts in relationships is not what people are going to be to you but what you will choose to be to them. This book's inspiration is to help you appreciate people, and in doing so understand the connection between your destiny and the various forms of relationships that are available to you. It is essentially about how to form genuine, fulfilling, and lasting relationships. Within this book, I am also going to show you how you can release the power of God available to you so that, through forgiveness, you can reach great heights in life and fulfil the very purpose for your creation.

Giving men and women the resources and tools they need to succeed in life and fulfil the reason for which they were created.

CHAPTER 1

The More Excellent Way

"But earnestly desire the best gifts. And yet I show you a more excellent way" (**1 Corinthians 12:31, NKJV**).

"Though I speak with the tongues of men and of angels, but have not love, I have become sounding brass or a clanging cymbal. And though I have the gift of prophecy, and understand all mysteries and all knowledge, and though I have all faith, so that I could remove mountains, but have not love, I am nothing. And though I bestow all my goods to feed the poor, and though I give my body to be burned, but have not love, it profits me nothing. And now abide faith, hope, love, these three; but the greatest of these is love" (**1 Corinthians 13:1-3, 13, NKJV**).

The more excellent way is the way of love. Love is superior to manifestations of supernatural power. As fantastic as all the gifts of the Spirit are (and we know that God desires for us to walk in them so we can be a blessing to people), love is superior and more important than all of them. We know that the devil can and does imitate the gifts; there are so many spectacular manifestations out there in the world. Satan can perform them but he cannot walk in love, because love is the very essence and nature of God. The Bible says, "God is love" (**1 John 4:8**). The great news is that all born again people have the ability to love, because the love of God is shed abroad or implanted in their heart by the Holy Spirit (**Romans 5:5**). In reference to love, the Bible makes it clear that "he who does not love does not know God, for God is love (**1 John 4:7-8**). The believer in Christ is not lacking the capacity to love. God desires that whatever we do should be motivated by love; love is to be the guide to the new creation. Whatever we do that is not born out of love will not receive God's recognition or blessing; it is a waste. We must be people who love people irrespective of their background, colour, race, or religious affiliations. We are not called to only love the brethren (i.e., those who profess the same religious convictions as ourselves), but rather we are called to love all human beings. We are not to treat anyone as an enemy, no matter what they do to us. Others may see us and even treat us as their enemies, but we are not to behave in that manner.

Sincerely ask yourself the following questions: "Why do I do the things I do? Why am I involved with the people I am involved with?" We all do the things we do for several reasons. People do certain things just so they can seem to be involved (these are identity seekers). Some people do things to impress people or make somebody happy (these are pleasers). Some do what they do because somebody else is doing the same thing (these are followers). Some people are purely interested in the material or financial gain they can get from being involved. These people work primarily for profit (they are profit centred). Some people get involved in something because of the honour or prestige that is in the job (these are position centred).

Some people do what they do because they love Jesus, and for His love's sake, some have left their home and family and gone to a strange land; they lived in tents, caves, or huts, forsaking the pleasures of life. Some have sold their property, emptied their bank accounts, and given all they had to feed the poor; others gave their all to the Lord in order to build a kingdom on the earth for Him. Some rejected, in the face of death, the offer of freedom in exchange for their lives and instead chose to die; they were beheaded, hanged, or burnt alive because of their commitment to Him (they found the love of God within and allowed it to rule over their hearts and minds; they became selfless).

We know that God wants our dealings, gifts, and services to come out of love, love for Him first and for the people He has called us to minister to. The Bible says, *"Whatever you do in word or deed, do all in the name of the Lord Jesus . . . do it heartily, as to the Lord and not men"* (**Colossians 3:17, 23-25**). The only way to do a thing as to God is with a heart of love. If you want to do anything for God and you want Him to accept it, then your love for Him must be your sole motivation. If you want to do anything for anybody and you want God to recognise or reward it, then it must come from a heart filled with love. If you really love somebody, you will find nothing too great to sacrifice for them. If you love God, nothing will be too great to give to Him. Do not serve God primarily because you want Him to bless you. He will definitely bless you when you serve Him, but rather serve Him because you love Him. This does not only apply to God, but to people as well. Whatever you want to do for people, do it out of love. Anything that is not born out of love really does not count in God's scheme of things.

The Greatest Is Love

> *"And now abideth faith, hope, charity, these three; but the greatest of these is charity"* (**1 Corinthians 13:13**).

In the above scripture, the reference to "charity" also means "love"; it does not mean being charitable or being a giving person, it refers to love in its entirety. The three pillars that hold the church together, which connect the church to the Lord and determine the quality of the believers' spirituality, are faith, hope, and love. Every believer needs to understand that anything we do outside these three will not stand the test on the day of judgement. Faith, hope, and love are very important in our relationship with the Lord and in our existence as a church:

remove one of these pillars and everything we hold to as values falls to pieces. Of these three pillars, the Bible states that love is the greatest. In other words, love is superior to both faith and hope. Our faith and our hope are anchored by love. Our faith and hope receive life from love. Without love faith does not work; without love hope fails, it turns into disappointment.

Faith, hope, and love all work corporately, but love is the most excellent or the greatest of them because both faith and hope need love to produce results. The way these three work is that whenever you hear the Word of God, faith rises in your spirit, for faith comes through hearing the Word of God (**Romans 10:17**). When faith rises in your spirit, hope (expectation) rises too. As a result of faith rising in your heart, you start to anticipate something happening, and you look out for it; that is hope. However, your faith and hope will need you to walk in love, the God kind of love, in order for you to experience the physical manifestation of what you are expecting to happen. Look what the scriptures are saying:

> *"For in Christ Jesus neither circumcision nor uncircumcision avails anything, but faith working through love"* (**Galatians 5:6**, **NKJV**).

> *"Now hope does not disappoint, because the love of God has been poured out in our hearts by the Holy Spirit who was given to us"* (**Romans 5:5**, **NKJV**).

Only where love is will faith find expression and hope not disappoint. Your faith and hope will be dead without love; it is the love of God in your heart that keeps them alive and empowers them to produce results. The Bible says in **2 Corinthians 13:5**, *"Examine yourselves as to whether you are in the faith. Test yourselves. Do you not know yourselves, that Jesus Christ is in you? Unless indeed you are disqualified."* The yard stick for that examination is love. If love is not established in your heart, your relationship with the Lord counts to nothing, your faith is dead, and all your spiritual devotion amounts to nothing.

See **1 John 4:7-12, 20-21**. Without love in you, your prayers will definitely be hindered. The very nature of God is love, so when you allow the love of God to soften your heart and you allow it to be the motivation in everything you do, you will be walking in the nature of God. When God says to be like Him, or to be followers of Him as dear children, He is saying that you should walk in love (see **Ephesians 5:1-2; 1 John 4:7-8; Matthew 5:46-48**).

As you walk in love, you act like God. If you walk in His nature, you will not walk in defeat, you will walk in victory. When you walk in love, you are walking in freedom (**1 John 3:14, 15**). In the way of love, you are free from bondage, you are free from fear, and the weapons of the enemy against you will not prosper. In the way of love, you can conquer enemies, you heap coals of fire on their head, and you can win them back as friends. In the way of love, you cannot be overcome by Satan; no demon can afflict you and prevail against you. See **Romans 12:20, 21**. In love, you are covered in God's fullness, His eternal life works in you, and you cannot be defeated (**Ephesians 3:17-19**). There are three Greek words that have been translated as love, but they actually mean three different kinds of love.

Eros

Eros is the kind of love that exists between two people of the opposite sex; it is sexual in nature. Eros is also a gift from God. You need it to connect with a woman or man you want to be with; you need it to form a lasting relationship and make a great marriage. What happens in a marriage relationship, for instance, is that the man first of all sees the woman, or vice versa, gets attracted, and desires to share his life with her, and this is because he finds her attractive. She is beautiful, holds herself well, and looks sexy. She is the kind of woman he can die for. On the other hand, she wants him too because he is masculine, is handsome, and has a good job, and she thinks he can protect her. Eros involves sexual attraction and is necessary for a healthy relationship between a man and woman. Eros is good, it is a gift to humans, and we need it to want to be with the opposite sex; however, it is not the excellent way. Eros is not the excellent way; it can fail, and that is why we see a lot of separations, betrayals, and divorces amongst those who once appeared as great lovers. We have seen husbands murdering their wives and vice versa for some selfish reasons. We need Eros to make a great marriage relationship, but Eros alone cannot make a lasting marriage relationship.

Phileo

Phileo is the kind of love that exists between friends or within a family. It is the kind of love that exists between parents and children, between the children, between the children and uncles or aunts, and between cousins. Family members always care for each other and are willing to support and protect each other because they are related; they are a family. Phileo is only about the family, which is the connecting string. Here, an outsider cannot enjoy what an insider can get. Phileo helps to keep family close and together, but it is also not the excellent way; it can fail in challenging times. It has not got the capacity to deal with greed, selfishness, rivalry, and strife in the family. Good families have scattered before because of clumsy, stupid reasons. Children have murdered their parents out of selfishness. Phileo is great, but it is not the excellent way.

Agape

Agape is the kind of love that originates from God. It is actually the very nature of God; the very thing that makes God who He is. This is the kind of love that God demonstrated towards us when He gave us Jesus (**John 3:16**). This is the kind of love that Jesus demonstrated when He gave His life for the redemption of humankind (**John 15:13**), and this is the kind of love that He commands us to show to one another. It is the new commandment Jesus gave to His body, the church:

"A new commandment I give unto you, that ye love one another; as I have loved you, that ye also love one another" (**John 13:34**).

Agape is superior to all kinds of love; it does not love somebody because there is a relationship, either sexual or biological, that connects them together. Agape loves without strings attached. Agape is never mindful of nationality, colour, status, behavioural flaws, or shortcomings, and it is never self-centred. Agape is the unconditional love. This is the more excellent way, the God kind of love (**John 3:16, Romans 5:8**).

The Nature and Ways of Agape

Agape is love that has no deception (love without dissimulation). See **Romans 12:9**. In other words, it is not superficial or fake, it is genuine, and it comes from the heart. It is not the kind that smiles at you and says good things about you when you are there but says something else when you are not there. There is no hypocrisy in agape. Agape is pure (**1 Peter 1:22**). It never wishes anybody evil, it does not think evil of anybody, and it is not selfish. For instance, agape does not go into a relationship just for fun, for sex, or for wealth. Its motive is pure and not self-centred. There is a need for Eros in every marriage, but as Christians, phileo or Eros should not be the only factors in our relationships. Agape, the God kind of love, should be the determining factor in every believer's heart and relationships. Our relationships are likely going to disintegrate in the face of tough challenges if we do not allow agape, the God kind of love, to form in our hearts for the people we are in relationship with.

Agape is fervent (**1 Peter 1:22**). Being fervent means agape loves with intensity, passion, and dedication. Agape can be persistent; it never gives up on people. Agape loves no matter what happens (**Hebrews 13:1, Proverbs 17:17**). Sometimes the people you love a lot are the ones that will hurt you the most, but agape keeps on loving, no matter what. Some people may never even respond to your love, while some of them may be blunt enough to tell you how disgusting they think you are and how they do not need you in their lives; even with that, agape keeps on loving, it is persistent, it never gives up.

Agape is fearless. The Bible says, *"There is no fear in love; but perfect love casteth out fear: because fear hath torment. He that feareth is not made perfect in love"* (**1 John 4:18**). The God kind of love is the perfect love, when it is allowed to dwell in us; it drives out fear, especially the fear of what men can do to us. When you are walking in love with your enemy, the fear of what he might do to you will be subdued. If you love somebody with the perfect love, you will not live with him in fear. I mean you will not nurse the idea that one day he is going to hurt you. In agape, you are secured, assured, and will never live with the person in fear because there is no fear in love. In agape, you will not have the fear of losing the person you love to somebody else, because there is security in the agape love.

Agape enables you to freely release people to pursue their dream, to step out and do what is their passion and not be afraid of losing them. Also with agape love in your heart, you will not be afraid of what people will think about your relationship with somebody; you do not care about people secretly so people do not know you feel that way for them. You need be careful, ladies, with men who come round saying, "I love you, I want us to be together, hopefully we will get married someday, but let's keep this between us. I don't want anybody knowing we are together." I have seen a lot of that in my work as pastor, and I can tell you it always ends in hurt and heartbreak. If he is not confident enough to make it public, he needs to leave you alone until he is.

Agape is selfless (**1 Corinthians 13:4-6, John 15:13**). Being selfless means the God kind of love places the needs of others first; it seeks to protect the interests of others first and seeks to make others happy, even at the expense of itself. Agape makes sacrifices for others; it is able to go all out and completely out of its way to help somebody else. Agape is not a convenient giver, it is a sacrificial and selfless giver. It can easily make itself uncomfortable so somebody can find comfort. It can lay down its life so somebody can live. The God kind of love places others first, it will not seek to rise at the expense of its neighbour, it will not take advantage of its neighbour, its joy is in making others feel great. The motivation in agape is not about what it can gain out of something but about what it can contribute—what it can bring to make a difference.

Agape does no ill to its neighbour (**Romans 13:10**). The God kind of love has no wickedness within it. It does not wish anybody evil, no matter who the person is or what he is doing. The God kind of love will not go out to do anybody evil. Where agape is found, the people will not intentionally say or do anything that will harm or hurt another person. They will not seek to destroy another man's image or reputation. They will not think evil of anyone and will not wish another evil. They will not defraud or take advantage of anyone. They will not stand in the way of another's success; they will not fail to contribute what is in their power to give in order to help them succeed. They will not stand in the way of others or withhold a blessing due to them.

Agape does no ill to its neighbour. Sometimes, people hold back from being a source of help in reaction to an offence, but that is not the nature of the God kind of love. Agape, the God kind of love, forgives (**Proverbs 10:12, 1 Corinthians 13:5**). It has the capacity to forgive people and let go of anything done against them. Actually one of the practical ways the love of God is demonstrated is in the area of forgiveness. It is practically impossible to be walking in love, the God kind of love, and not forgive. We are going to be looking at forgiveness in more detail in Chapter 6. In the love of God, you will find no offence too great to forgive; you will not hold grudges, malice, or bitterness against anybody, no matter what they may have done against you.

Agape Is a Generous Giver

Another practical way that agape is demonstrated is in giving. You cannot be walking in love and be able to hold back what is good from somebody in need. God also demonstrated His love towards us by giving us Jesus (**John 3:16**). Jesus demonstrated His love towards us when He gave of Himself to redeem us from sin. Love never holds back, it gives freely and lavishly. Agape is extravagant in giving; it gives even to an enemy and not only to friends (**Romans 12:9, 20-21**). As I said earlier, agape treats no one as an enemy. It deals with an enemy as it would a friend. It is not selective in showing generosity; it is good to all. See **Matthew 5:43-48, Ephesians 6:12, 1 Peter 5:8**. Agape serves (**Galatians 5:13**). The person who is walking in the God kind of love is available and accessible to people. Agape seeks to serve people first rather than be served. You see, with agape, no matter your name, your status, or your résumé, you do not become too important to serve people, and the class or social standing of the people you are serving does not matter.

Agape is the kind of love Jesus walked in here on earth. Jesus was the embodiment of God's love, and we see that He made Himself available and accessible to all. His life touched both the rich and the poor, Jews, Samaritans, and Gentiles. He reached out to serve the widow, the sinner, the prostitute, the blind, the lame, and the outcast. He made Martha, Mary, and Lazarus His friends, and He travelled a two-night journey to Bethany to serve them when Lazarus died. He went to raise him from death to life so God would be glorified (**John 11:1-45**). He accepted Zacchaeus, even though He knew he was a renowned tax collector, a sinner. He let Zacchaeus interrupt His journey to an important meeting when He went to dine with him. He wanted even Zacchaeus to have an experience of salvation (**Luke 19:1-10**). In the midst of His busy schedule, He responded to a call for help from Bartimæus, the son of Timæus, even though he was a nobody; everyone thought Jesus should be too busy and that He was too important to be interrupted by a man like him. However, Jesus thought Bartimæus was also worthy of His attention.

Jesus wanted him to have his sight back (**Mark 10:45-52**). He taught people the Word of God as well as fed them with bread. He stooped down and washed His disciples' feet and dried them with a towel to show them how servanthood is honourable.

The Honour and Joy of Servanthood

It is a privilege to be at a place where we can serve people, meet needs in their lives, and help them to be their best and fulfil their purpose here on the earth. The heart and life of servanthood is a superior way of life, and it is more rewarding than any other thing; however, it is rare in our generation. The emphasis among believers today is more on what we can get from God or what He can empower us to achieve for ourselves rather than on what we can give out to be a blessing. That is reflected in our manner of prayers and in the motive behind the offerings or tithes that we give to God. The God kind of love is what can motivate us to live a selfless life, seek for the best in people, commit to serve people, not for what we can gain from it, but purely because we are willing to give of what we have to help bring the best in people.

Service that is motivated by the love of God transforms people, it gives life to a community, and it reflects the nature and character of God. The life of service does not compete to be better than its neighbour; instead, it paves the way for its neighbour to rise to success. The servant attitude means living your life for others, working to make other people comfortable and happy in life. Agape, the God kind of love, does not seek its interest first; its interest is to make its neighbour a better person. Its interest is not what it can get but what it can give. The Bible says:

> "That so labouring ye ought to support the weak, and to remember the words of the Lord Jesus, how he said, It is more blessed to give than to receive" (**Acts 20:35**).

We are all called to be servants to all people; we are to labour to support the weak and help the poor. We are to help to bring joy to the oppressed, deliver hope to the downtrodden, and introduce Jesus to our lost world. To be a true servant, you must get rid of self-centredness. You are not going to be a good servant if all you care about is your own welfare. You must get rid of your competitive attitude; everyone has it, but yours needs to go. You cannot let go of what you have that can help make people better if all you want is to be better than them. You will also need to consider yourself of no reputation (**Philippians 2:6-7**). That was what Jesus did that enabled Him to become a servant. You must come to that place where your educational qualifications, social status, family name, or background do not count, the place where you can sacrifice them all to Jesus. You are not going to be able to serve the people that you think are beneath you, because you consider yourself to be more important than they are.

You cannot be of service to the people you consider as servants. There should be nobody that you should find inferior and unworthy of being served by you. When Jesus stooped down and washed His disciples' feet, He was trying to communicate that it is actually the leader, the better, the richer that should be of service to the led, the weaker, and the poor, not the other way round. As it is written, *"But Jesus called them unto him, and said, Ye know that the princes of the Gentiles exercise dominion over them, and they that are great exercise authority upon them. But it shall not be so among you: but whosoever will be great among you, let him be your minister; And whosoever will be chief among you, let him be your servant"* (**Matthew 20:25-27**).

CHAPTER 2

The Power of Believers' Fellowship

"And let us consider one another to provoke unto love and to good works: Not forsaking the assembling of ourselves together, as the manner of some is; but exhorting one another: and so much the more, as ye see the day approaching" **(Hebrews 10:24-25).**

One of the great gifts that God gave believers is the institution of the believers' congregational gathering and fellowship. The scriptures clearly show that God called us into relationship with Him and to the fellowship of the brethren. Some people have taught that to be in a relationship with God is not about going to church. They say that as long as you and God are in a relationship, then that is all that is required, but that is not scriptural. Although Christianity is not just about going to church meetings, God still ordained that believers should meet in a community on a regular basis for prayer, corporate worship, and fellowship. I am aware that there are people who dislike church meetings for many different reasons, which include that they have been hurt in church before, while others dislike church because they were not brought up going to church, so it is alien to them. In a similar category are those who dislike church because they find it boring or irrelevant or think the service is too long.

However, the truth remains that when we come into a relationship with God, we are meant to orientate ourselves regarding godly principles, His values, and the way His kingdom is designed to function. All believers need to understand how our kingdom functions, and they must align themselves, their thought processes, and their behaviour to it. I have seen that some people want to follow God but only on their own terms, or in a way that suits them, but it is not so with God. To follow God, it must be on His own terms not ours. And He has said:

> "Consider one another to provoke unto love and to good works: Not forsaking the assembling of ourselves together, as the manner of some is" (**Hebrews 10:24-25).**

Believers' fellowship is the way God has designed this kingdom. The word "fellowship" is from the Greek word κοινωνία (*koinonia*), which means to contribute to the community, distribute from what they have and to have communion with God or with people. From its meaning, you can see that fellowship is more than just believers coming together; yes, it is about coming together, but for the aim of achieving something, not just for the sake of it. Believers benefit a lot when they come together in fellowship. In fellowship, we establish friendship or a relationship with other believers, and through that friendship, our lives are impacted.

To get the maximum of what God has deposited inside other people, we must come into fellowship with them and must develop that relationship. Therefore, God ordained fellowship so that through it, we can connect with the people He has anointed to be a blessing to us. You have got something that can change somebody's life, and God wants to use what He has deposited in you to bless somebody. You need to become more aware of the people around you and look out for what you can do to make their lives more comfortable. Most times, we all need the help of somebody to find our bearing in life, which is why the Bible says:

"Two are better than one; because they have a good reward for their labour. For if they fall, the one will lift up his fellow: but woe to him that is alone when he falleth; for he hath not another to help him up. Again, if two lie together, then they have heat: but how can one be warm alone? And if one prevail against him, two shall withstand him; and a threefold cord is not quickly broken" (**Ecclesiastes 4:9-12**)

The other importance of being part of a fellowship is that it makes you accountable to one another within that fellowship. In a believers' fellowship, we put ourselves in a position where we can be taught, instructed, corrected, and even rebuked when we get it wrong. This helps to keep us on the right track. Some people do not want to be taught, corrected, or instructed. They think they know too much and require no help. They want to live their life and want nobody telling them how to live it. They call it independence. But it is dangerous to put yourself in a position where nobody can talk to you to bring you to order, even when you are missing it. A lot of people have ended relationships and marriages that would have made them great; some have quit jobs, left churches, walked out of a place which is connected to their destiny because they would not allow anyone to be in a position of authority to speak into their life.

God ordained the church fellowship so that believers can be constantly guided, both theologically and doctrinally, and also instructed in righteousness. That way we are protected from error (**Acts 2:42**). It is also true that none of us is perfect; we all sometimes commit sin in one way or the other. Sometimes there are sins we cannot confess because we do not even know they exist. You see, there are many things we don't do right and are not even aware of, but because we are continuing in fellowship with the brethren, the Bible says the blood of Jesus is constantly purifying us from all sin (**Psalm 133:1-3**), just by remaining in fellowship. The writer of John puts it this way:

"But if we walk in the light, as he is in the light, we have fellowship one with another, and the blood of Jesus Christ his Son cleanseth us from all sin" (**1 John 1:7**).

The Place of Blessing and Life for Evermore

God designed our place of fellowship to be a place where blessings flow, a place where emotional healing, relationship healing, and even physical healing takes place. It is designed to be a place where people don't feel lonely; don't get depressed; don't feel rejected, judged, and uncared for.

"Behold, how good and how pleasant it is for brethren to dwell together in unity! It is like the precious ointment upon the head, that ran down upon the beard, even Aaron's beard: that went down to the skirts of his garments; As the dew of Hermon, and as the dew that descended upon the mountains of Zion: for there the Lord commanded the blessing, even life for evermore." (**Psalm 133:1-3**).

If our fellowship is genuine, we won't struggle with sharing our worries, needs, and fears with each other, because in fellowship we walk in light, and where there is light, there will be no darkness but friendship and support instead (**1 John 1:6-7**). You find that people will genuinely share their challenges when they know they are not going to be judged or undermined. People are not going to freely share their worries if they think the whole world is going to hear about it. People will only share if they can trust and can see that help is available. In fellowship, we are to share with others all the good things of life that the Lord has blessed us with. It is important that you come to believers' gatherings not only to receive but with something to give. It is always better to give than to receive. Never think that you have nothing to give, nobody is created empty, you are blessed, and there is something that you have that can help to transform somebody's life; it's only that you have not realised it. As you come for fellowship, be on the lookout for an opportunity to be a blessing. We are to help to meet each other's emotional, spiritual, and material needs. The early believers understood the importance of sharing and engaged in it devotedly. Paul the apostle writes to Timothy and says:

> "Charge them that are rich in this world, that they be not highminded, nor trust in uncertain riches, but in the living God, who giveth us richly all things to enjoy; That they do good, that they be rich in good works, ready to distribute, willing to communicate; Laying up in store for themselves a good foundation against the time to come, that they may lay hold on eternal life" (**1 Timothy 6:17-19**).

As we start to effectively fellowship amongst the brethren, we will find that we are fulfilling what God has said in **Galatians 6:2** concerning bearing one another's burden, and as we learn to bear each other's burden, we will be provoking each other to love as the Bible has said to do (**Hebrews 10:24**). We are to also share with each other in spiritual things like praying for each other, sharing in the understanding of the Word together, sharing in prophecies and revelations we have received, and using our spiritual gifts for the edification of each other. We can also receive healing, favour, deliverance, breakthrough, new direction, and the like when in fellowship more easily than when we are by ourselves.

When we come together, the Lord says He will be with us, and in His presence, there is fullness of joy (**Psalm 16:11**). The Bible also says that "where the Spirit of God is, there is liberty" (**2 Corinthians 3:17**). These verses mean that in the believers' gathering, God releases joy, He destroys bondages, and all limitations are lifted; God's presence within His people makes it so. The anointing or God's enabling power is always available when believers are in fellowship. Expect something to happen to you any time you come into the fellowship of the brethren.'

Good and Pleasant Place

A good and pleasant place is the place where brethren dwell together in unity. True fellowship involves being in one accord. It is the state of being in one accord that makes believers' fellowship good and pleasant. Where there is true fellowship, there won't be division, competition, strife, malice, or jealousy. Where there is true fellowship, we will all prefer each other in love; we will have each other's best interests at heart and will be supportive of each other. Where there is one accord, people don't stand in the way of each other; instead, they want to reach out to help the other person become better and find more fulfilment in life. Where there is one accord, people work to keep and to protect the bond, they don't judge, they don't carry unhealthy rumours, and they don't put a seed of discord between brethren.

We know that a kingdom divided against itself cannot stand. When we are united, we are strong. When we are united, we are able to achieve more than we would as individuals. The Bible says that one can chase a thousand, two will put ten thousand to flight (**Deuteronomy 32:30**). When the devil causes disunity and splits in a group of people, he has succeeded in limiting their potential. There is something you cannot achieve on your own without the help of somebody else. Unity does not only mean agreeing with people on their ideology and lifestyle. The fact that we all are different means that we will approach things in a different way. Unity is about having appreciation for our differences and seeing this as a gift. Unity is about respecting other people's point of views, valuing them, and allowing them to express it. Unity is about agreeing to a common cause and contributing to make it happen; it is about making every effort to live peaceably and in harmony with people. God desires that we live in peace with all people (**Hebrews 12:14).** God desires that we be reconciled to all men, even to our enemies (**Proverbs 16:7**).

You need to understand that everybody the Lord brings into your life or your way is very crucial in the plan of God for you. There is something, even about your enemies, that you can benefit from if you can be reconciled to them, and that is why you are never to pray for your enemies to die, but that God will restore peace to them instead. Remember that your problems with them were caused by Satan the enemy; he likes to split people because he knows what potential can be generated when you are together. Unity is about sticking with somebody in both good times and rough times. To achieve unity, we all need to accept the truth that everybody the Lord brings into our lives or our way is very crucial in His plan for us. If where you are is God's will for you, then the people who are in that place are relevant to you. God put you there in their midst because they have something to contribute to His plan for your life.

When we do not know how to relate with people, we are going to have a fight with them and disintegrate. As a result, what God intends to achieve through us and them would be interrupted. There are people who have lost their jobs because they could not cope with colleagues. Some people have split with their spouses because they could not cope with their differences. Some people have moved out of a neighbourhood because of a difficult neighbour; they could not exercise tolerance. Some people have also left the church because they weren't agreeing with another member; they were offended in some way. We cannot deny that some people are very difficult to deal with. Human beings are generally very complex; they can be selfish, arrogant, inconsiderate, and competitive. However, there is nobody that is impossible to work alongside, for the new creation.

Multicultural and Multiracial Is God's Idea

God is dynamic, is creative, and has a beautiful mind. He made the world beautiful and colourful. He made humans white, red, brown, and black, and upon all He has put glory and honour. The world is colourful, bright and beautiful; God enjoys the flavour and diversity that we all bring. We may look different from each other, but we all are the same, created to be connected and relevant to each other. It is therefore of utmost importance that we all learn to place value on all people irrespective of their colour, race, or background. Multiculturalism is God's idea. He will bring you into the life of people of different races, colours, and backgrounds, all endowed with the ability to make a contribution to our world and to your life. That is the picture that He has of the church:

> *"And they sang a new song saying: You are worthy to take the scroll and to open its seals, because you were slain, and with your blood you purchased men for God from every tribe and language and people and Nation'"* (**Revelation 5:9**, **NIV**).

> *"After this I beheld, and, lo, a great multitude, which no man could number, of all nations, and kindreds, and people, and tongues, stood before the throne, and before the Lamb, clothed with white robes, and palms in their hands; And cried with a loud voice, saying, Salvation to our God which sitteth upon the throne, and unto the Lamb"* (**Revelation 7:9-10**).

The church is a group of people that have been redeemed by the blood of Jesus from different tongues, nations, peoples, and cultures. Cultural diversity is God's dream of the church. It is the heart of God that in His kingdom there should be people of all nations. God desires to link you up with people from all nations. It is a fact that where several cultures meet together, there are bound to be differences and a clash of cultures. There will definitely be things about the other people and their culture that you may not be accustomed to, and in which case, you might feel very uncomfortable with. It is very possible that some people's mannerisms or ways of doing things, if different from your culture group, may put you off or appear to you as being abnormal. It is okay to be different; diversity makes our world interesting and exciting. It would be dull and boring if we were all the same.

We all see our world and behave differently. We all have the tendency to stereotype people, but we must learn to connect with the individual and every person as being unique. For instance, it is said that Nigerians talk loud, laugh a lot, and can appear very blunt, rude, and forceful. English people can appear very polite but scheming and undermining. Zimbabweans can appear unserious, timid, and withdrawn. Ghanaians are not very much different from Nigerians, except that they can be nicer. Americans are known for being excessive, arrogant, generous yet selfish. That is stereotyping, seeing people as being the same and behaving in the same way simply because they come from a particular race or culture group.

The assertion that every white person is a racist, every black person is an ignorant criminal, every Arab is a terrorist, and every Asian is crafty and corrupt is a fallacy. Stereotyping only promotes prejudices. Prejudice is when we judge people even before we get to meet them, which in turn leads to discrimination. You cannot have a fruitful relationship with people and enjoy the most of it if you approach them with a prejudged mind-set. To maintain God's own vision of a church/world with people from different tongues, nations, peoples, and cultures, we all must see the good in all people, knowing that there is always something we can learn from each other. As we learn to forbear one another in love, we must endeavour to keep the unity of the Spirit in the bond of peace, and we must put on charity for one another and allow the peace of God to rule in our heart.

Forbearing one another in love is about being patient with people, not being judgemental, being forgiving, and being tolerant. Being able to accept, connect, and fellowship with people, without any inhibition, irrespective of who they are or where they come from. There is a lot of cultural prejudice and stereotyping out there in the world. And it saddens me that it exists in the church as well. The church is both culturally and racially segregated. We all want to be with our own kind of people or people of our colour. We can't stand each other; we are easily agitated. I think the church is even more segregated than the world of our time. Sunday is the most divisive day of the week, because that is the day that Africans, Asians, black people, and Caucasians all part ways in the name of God. We must fight segregation of any sort in the church and in our communities; we must, as the word of God has said, endeavour to keep the unity of the spirit in the bond of peace.

To endeavour means to make effort or to work hard to achieve something. You as an individual must see cultural diversity in church as God's own heartfelt passion. You as an individual must see church with cultural diversity as your kind of place. If you don't you are only going to stick with your kind of people, wanting things done your own kind of way, and getting irritated with everybody that is different. You as an individual must make effort to cross cultural boundaries by consciously and intentionally reaching out to people of other cultures and building relationships with them.

Don't just hang around with your kind. You are not multicultural at heart if all the people you hang around with are from your own culture. Learn to show respect and appreciation for our diversity; appreciate other people and their ways of doing things. We are different and do things differently; we relate and talk differently. Don't be dogmatic about your cultural viewpoint; we are all culturally different, but learning to accommodate that is most important. You need to intentionally avoid sectionalism. Be graciously tolerant; don't always be put off by the other person's ways of doing things.

You can achieve unity with whosoever God puts you in contact with

"The steps of a good man are ordered by the Lord: and he delighteth in his way" (**Psalm 37:23**).

All the people God will bring into your life are relevant to your destiny, irrespective of the problems they might be in or their excesses. Some people can be really difficult to relate with; however, God will not bring you in their way, no matter how complicated they are, without giving you the grace to accommodate them and together achieve that which He had destined. To achieve unity, we must treat people we come in contact with as being special and show that we enjoy being, living, and working with them. Anybody who really desires to achieve unity must be easily entreated and never pay evil for evil. The book of Romans says:

"Recompense to no man evil for evil. Provide things honest in the sight of all men. If it be possible, as much as lieth in you, live peaceably with all men. Dearly beloved, avenge not yourselves, but rather give place unto wrath: for it is written, Vengeance is mine; I will repay, saith the Lord" (**Romans 12:17-19**).

Being easily entreated means you are somebody who easily makes room for peace and reconciliation. You must always recognise when somebody is sorry and let it go. Always let it go when you can see that there is remorse. Don't go on and on, control your tongue. Don't let the sun set on your anger. When somebody says they're sorry, make it the end of the matter. Don't be somebody who is difficult to make peace with, don't be the hard and difficult type, be easily entreated (**James 3:17-18).** If you can't forgive, you will always be fighting people, and when you do fight, even when you are right, it will still appear as if you are quarrelsome and unkind. If you cannot forgive, you are at risk to destroy the beautiful things you have developed over many years. If you don't know how to subdue hurts and bitterness, especially, no matter what is done to you, they are going to ruin you.

You must know that nobody is perfect. Therefore, there is no one person that God is going to bring into your life that will be perfect and not capable of making a blunder. The people you are dealing with will make mistakes, offend you in some way, shape, or form, or do things in a way you don't appreciate. That may happen and not necessarily because they set out to hurt you, but because of the human factor. You must learn to forgive at all times and forgive everything. If you can't forgive, you will fight with people, and you are likely to use your mouth to want to destroy them. You will want to show the person who offended you that they are a bad person, and you are going to help them walk away from you. Unforgiveness brings scattering. Unforgiveness is a destroyer. Your ability to genuinely forgive will endear you to people.

In many cases, people separate (even married couples) and go their separate ways, not because they are not meant to be together or meant for each other but because people can offend and hurt each other. If you don't know how to deal with hurts, your life is going to end up like a shipwreck. Many have interrupted destiny: many have divorced, closed down companies they started, quit jobs, and walked away from people they once loved, solely because they have been unable to genuinely forgive. Also many have killed, maimed, and betrayed people they once loved because they were hurt and did not know how to deal with it in a godly way. One of God's ways of tackling challenges is prayer. The Apostle Paul writes to Timothy and says:

> "I exhort therefore, that, first of all, supplications, prayers, intercessions, and giving of thanks, be made for all men; For kings, and for all that are in authority; that we may lead a quiet and peaceable life in all godliness and honesty. For this is good and acceptable in the sight of God our Saviour" (**1 Timothy 2:1-3**).

Prayer can help to create the right perspective, and it can bring God into every situation you want Him to be involved in. Remember, Satan likes to spoil what you have got with people; he knows there is something in everybody you relate with that can benefit you. To overcome your enemy Satan, you must learn to pray for your relationships every day. Pray for the people you care about, for God to help them see things from a clear and more positive perspective. Pray for God to lead you to the people who are going to have a part to play in your life and vice versa.

Avoid Being Judgemental or Negative

> *"If there be therefore any consolation in Christ, if any comfort of love, if any fellowship of the Spirit, if any bowels and mercies, Fulfil ye my joy, that ye be likeminded, having the same love, being of one accord, of one mind. Let nothing be done through strife or vainglory; but in lowliness of mind let each esteem others better than themselves. Look not every man on his own things, but every man also on the things of others"* **(Philippians 2:1-4).**

A negative person is somebody who is a fault finder, always looking out for what is wrong in people or in a place. He is always complaining, thinks nothing seems to be right, always worries, and has a bad attitude. A person is judgemental when he is not patient, kind hearted, considerate, and gracious at the weakness of others. Learn to give people the long rope, knowing that we can all make mistakes. Pay more attention to their positive side than to their failings, and learn to talk to people respectfully. Nobody likes to be around anybody who is always looking for faults and makes them feel less than they are. This judgemental attitude can lead to unworthy feelings in the hearts of others.

People will come to you when you make them feel great, like they can fly. You inspire confidence in people when you don't judge them when they get it wrong but help to bring the best in them. People will feel free to share just about anything with you if they know you think highly of them. The best thing to do when things are not going right in your relationship with people is to pray for them and pray about the situation. Don't be quick to judge them. The best thing you can give somebody when he seems to be going off or getting it wrong is genuine prayer. When you are having it rough with people, learn to pray more. Prayer can help to create the right perspective and can bring God into the situation. Remember, Satan likes to spoil what you've got with somebody; he knows there is something in everybody that you relate with which can benefit you.

Pray for your relationships every day; pray for the people you care about, for God to help them see things in a positive way. You will enjoy better relationships with the people you pray for. Some issues that arise in relationships are better resolved in prayer. What a conference cannot deal with, prayer can (actually, you should not bring everything to a conference table). Learn to take issues to God in prayer and allow Him to take your burdens. Prayer also changes you. If you can pray about it, you are likely to see things differently, calm down, and even behave differently and appropriately towards that person (**1 Timothy 2:1-3).**

Be a Builder, Not a Whisperer

Your interest must always be to strengthen the brotherhood and not to scatter it. In being a builder, one of the things you must do is to be careful that anything you say to a brother is seasoned with salt and that it edifies. You also need to watch what you say to somebody about another person. Be mindful of your words to ensure that your words are not unhealthy to your listener, that they do not plant hatred, dislike, or disrespect for anybody else (**Proverbs 16:27-28).** By all means avoid getting involved in conversations that you are not clear about; don't say anything about anybody that you are not sure of. Don't say anything that you know will tarnish somebody's image; don't do anything that you know will make somebody lose respect for another person or even cause people to part. Watch the following scriptures:

> *"These six things doth the Lord hate: yea, seven are an abomination unto him: A proud look, a lying tongue, and hands that shed innocent blood, An heart that deviseth wicked imaginations, feet that be swift in running to mischief, A false witness that speaketh lies, and he that soweth discord among brethren"***(Proverbs 6:16-19).**

> *"Now I beseech you, brethren, mark them which cause divisions and offences contrary to the doctrine which ye have learned; and avoid them"* **(Romans 16:17).**

Show Yourself Friendly and Not Given to Unhealthy Competition

If you want to attract and keep friends, you've got to show yourself friendly. You can achieve that by lending a listening ear, by being there when you are needed the most, by showing appreciation for every help you get, by giving gifts, by sharing your time, by visiting, by planning dinner outings. If you are friendly, you will make and keep friends. To make and keep friends, you will also need to not take every offence too seriously, learn to forgive, be very kind and helpful, and never think you know better. There is always something you can learn from the other person. Remember, everybody is gifted and has something to offer. When you are showing that you are a friend, you are going to find that people stick with you.

You are not just going to walk away from people on the slightest provocation. Provocations will always come, but it is how you handle them that matters. I have seen provocation make many people walked away from destiny helpers and sabotage their destiny **(Proverbs 18:24).** It is said that a friend in need is a friend indeed. You know a genuine friend, not when everything is going okay for you but when you are completely messed up and they are still sticking with you. I have also seen that one of the things that separate brethren is jealousy and unhealthy competition. When all a brother wants to do is to shine and be better than the other, jealousy sets in, and they start to do anything they can to pull the other fellow down. They do things to rise and don't care about how they rise, even if it is at the expense of the other; it ought not to be so among brethren. The Bible urges us to be mindful of those things that can cause divisions (**James 3:16**). As such, we are encouraged to consider each other's interest first. Never measure your success in the light of another man's success if you don't want to create unhealthy competition.

Never see yourself as better than the other person and deserving of more than they are getting. You will only make room for jealousy and strife. Sometimes even in the church, people are envious of one another and go into competition with each other, not because they are zealous for the kingdom, but for vainglory (**Galatians 5:26**). I have seen a lot of that, even amongst pastors. This is terribly sad. What started as kingdom work is no longer about God and the glory of His kingdom; it is now all about what we can achieve for ourselves, what name we can make for ourselves. This is an absolute tragedy. The ministry must be about making God great and enlarging His kingdom. It should never be about us.

Understand Organisational Order and Ranks

> *"They shall run like mighty men; they shall climb the wall like men of war; and they shall march everyone on his ways, and they shall not break their ranks: Neither shall one thrust another; they shall walk every one in his path: and when they fall upon the sword, they shall not be wounded"* (**Joel 2:7-8**).

You see, there is a way everything works in every community, family, or organisation. When you violate the order of things, or break ranks, you make room for confusion, you create friction, and you upset the spirit of harmony. You must understand the order of things wherever God has put you; know how things operate there. Order is about doing things in an organised way, and ranking is about the chain of command. Every group or organisation has a way it functions. If you belong to a group, you need to understand the order of things, how they function there, and key in. Don't yoke yourself to any people and then violate the system. You will only cause confusion and disunity.

By not breaking ranks, it means you must understand and work under the authority in the place you find yourself functioning. When you start to do things your own way, and set aside what those who are leaders over you have put in place, when you start to think you know more than they do and you ignore authority, you are not only rebelling, you are practicing witchcraft, and you are a spoiler. If you disagree with an institution or the structure in place, the best thing to do is to come out of it. If you are staying, you have got to key in and subject yourself to the order of things. You need to subject yourself to authority. That is how to promote unity. See **1 Corinthians 14:40.**

CHAPTER 3

Developing Healthy and Fruitful Relationships

"Two are better than one; because they have a good reward for their labour. For if they fall, the one will lift up his fellow: but woe to him that is alone when he falleth; for he hath not another to help him up. Again, if two lie together, then they have heat: but how can one be warm alone? And if one prevail against him, two shall withstand him; and a threefold cord is not quickly broken" **(Ecclesiastes 4:9-12).**

Relationships are very relevant in this journey of life. They can empower you, inspire you, and help you to achieve destiny. They can also demoralise you, stall you, and ruin you. However, all of these will be dependent on the kind of relationships that you form. Relationship is more than being a mere acquaintance; it is more than just knowing somebody's name. It also goes deeper than just being part of a team or a community of people. Relationship is about being a part of somebody's life; it is about being connected to or having a bond with somebody. We all need people to achieve something in life. There are things you may never have until somebody comes into your life and gives it to you; your effort won't make it happen. There are places you may never go to until somebody comes into your life and takes you there. There are things you may never know until you meet somebody and he shows it to you. There may be someone you need to meet to get somewhere, but you may never meet him until another person introduces you to him.

We all need some people for us to become what God intended us to be. Our destiny is tied to people, that is how life is designed. That is why God said it is not good for man to be alone (**Genesis 2:18**). We are called of God to be salt and light to the world; we are called to be a blessing to the people we come in contact with. All of us can be a blessing, but we can only make a significant difference or impact in people's lives when we place value on people in our lives and we consciously build a relationship with them. It does greatly benefit us to be in a relationship with somebody, whether it is a marriage or friendship. It does not matter how good or smart or wealthy you think you are, you still need other people in your life; we all need people. With all that you have, if you are lonely, you can easily be a prey for depression and frustration.

The majority of people who attempt suicide are victims of depression or frustration, which more often than not was caused by loneliness or the loss of happiness and the pleasure of living. Many good things that happen to people come through human channels. God uses people to minister to people; you can never be better off on your own. If you look back, you would see that you are where you are today because at some point in your life, you met this person or that person who made a difference in your life. We must all learn to place a high value on relationships and consider those in our lives as gifts from God, very important and relevant to our journey and aspirations.

You Are Not Called to Everybody

You must know that every relationship has the potential to impact your life. However, for any relationship to develop and positively affect the people in that relationship, it must be nurtured and built upon God's principles. God's first principle is that our relationship with Him must come first; it must have priority over everything else in our lives. As such, no relationship that we have with anybody should replace or have a place above our relationship with Him. We are not to be with anybody at the expense of God. This is why you need to also know that you are not called to everybody; you cannot be relevant to everybody. However, it is your duty to find the people you are assigned to and develop a relationship with them. Knowing the right people is important, because not everybody around you is sent by God to you.

There are people who are Satan sent, sent to distract and trouble you. Satan likes to contradict and destroy God's purposes in our lives. He likes to send the wrong people into our lives, and he uses them to steal our peace, to make our lives bitter and miserable, and to disrupt our future. It is up to you to be able to identify such people and keep them out of your life. I am not saying to have nothing to do with them at all; no, you can find a way of being a blessing to them, but not to have an in-depth relationship with them. You also need to understand that just becau: e you are having it rough with your spouse, your fiancée, or your friend, it does not necessarily mean that you are in a relationship with the wrong person.

God did not make any two people alike. We are all made to be unique and different. God does not bring two people who are of the same nature or of the same temperament together (it would be boring and unprofitable if we were all the same). Often God brings two people together who are completely opposite. The purpose is so that they can both complement each other. It is natural to be in a relationship with somebody who does not always see things from your own point of view, who you do not always understand, and whose ideas always tend to conflict with yours. Even with that in mind, every person God has sent into your life has had something put into them by God for the working out of the purposes in your life. It will not be everything in the person that is good, because we are all flawed; however, it is God's plan to use both the good and the bad in the person to accomplish his purposes in your life. He has also given us His Holy Spirit to assist us in our weaknesses and strive for better relationships with those He has placed in our lives. See **Romans 8:26.**

However, if you are in a relationship with somebody, and you can see that he does not have respect for your God, and he likes to stand in the way of your relationship with God, if you can see that he really does not care about you, and all he is interested in is what he can get from you, if he likes to hurt you or stand in your way to increase, that person is not God sent (**2 Corinthians 6:14-18).** That is not the kind of person I will encourage you to have a relationship with. Remember, I am not saying to have nothing to do with them: you can have them in your life and be a blessing to them without being close. You must know that nobody is perfect, and the people that God is going to bring you into relationship with are never going to be perfect, so you will need to make room for faults. You are sometimes going to quarrel and disagree on some issues, but you must never let those arguments cause your relationship to break up.

Understand Your Background: It Helped in Forming Your Worldview

Your past experiences and opinion of yourself will to a large part affect your ability to form a stable, healthy relationship and maintain it in order to take it to a great height. In knowing who you really are, you need to look at your past and see what has shaped you, what helped to form your worldview and your behaviour. We know that behaviours are formed by our upbringing and life experiences. The things you have been through have helped to make you who you are today. The culture that you were raised in and the values that have been passed on to you by your parents have helped to form your worldview. We all behave in certain ways and may relate to people in certain ways because of our past and upbringing. I remember when I newly arrived in Sheffield in the UK, the home of my adoption, a lovely couple invited me to their home for lunch. I met the man in his office that day, and from there we went to their home.

When we arrived, the table was all set, and his lovely wife appeared so welcoming and friendly. However, when we sat down for the meal, I saw that what was on table were things like bread, cheese, some bacon, and salad. Initially, I presumed that that was meant to be the starter, but after we finished, they offered me coffee and that was it. I left their home that day really feeling that something went wrong and was wondering what it could be. I could not put my finger on anything, but I was really worried. It took me a while before I realised that was a typical British lunch meal; there were no issues whatsoever, and they did treat me well. Why did I feel the way I did? It was because of my worldview and the culture I was coming from. In the part of Africa I come from, what we had for lunch would be seen as a snack; I was seeing things from that worldview not from the view of the new culture I was in.

There are things in your past that can damage what you have with somebody if you do nothing about it. The family and way in which you were raised impacted you in a way you may not have realised. For instance, if you come from a greedy, quarrelsome family or if you were raised with beliefs that are unhealthy, you are highly likely to see these traits in your behaviour and dealings with people. It will be different if you come from a calm, cheerful, generous family. Also, if you experienced an abusive childhood, it is possible to be carrying a lack of trust and pain inside you and have a tendency to become abusive without even realising that your behaviour is abusive, as to you it may be the normal way. If you have seen your father beat your mother, you are more likely to beat your wife than someone who grew up with parents who were not abusive to each other.

I once was involved in praying and counselling with a couple whose marriage was at the verge of collapsing. The woman was having problems with her temper and was verbally and physically abusive to her husband. He had slept out many times or returned home very late at night, keeping busy at work just to avoid his wife. That did not help matters though, as it infuriated her the more. In the course of counselling, I discovered that she was raised in that environment too, for she had seen her mother insult and hit her father many times. She grew up not liking her mother very much and had told herself that she would never do what she saw her mother do to her own husband. Unfortunately, things degenerated in the house, and she found herself doing exactly what she hated.

Your background has impacted on your life in a way that you may not have realised. If you have been hurt in the past and have not truly and thoroughly dealt with it and put it completely behind you, it can continue to affect your life through the way that you relate to people. If you were betrayed before, you are likely to struggle with trusting people. If you were molested as a child, that can affect your relationship with your spouse in some way and can also affect how you raise your own children. It may make you an over-protective parent. You may think that every adult who comes visiting your home may do the same to your children, because it is still in your mind.

Everything that you have experienced in the past has the potential to affect what you have now, unless you deal with it and leave it in the past. Nobody ever makes any meaningful progress in life with his eyes behind him. You need to look closely at what has influenced your makeup, bring it before the Lord, and then deal with it once and for all. That is part of the change that Jesus will like to happen to you so you can regain power over your destiny and so nothing can limit you.

The Value You Put on Yourself Reflects in Your Relationships

A negative minded person does not only have a poor impression of himself, he might also have a bad attitude towards people and a poor approach to life's challenges. The first thing to do in tackling a negative mind-set is to have an understanding of your value and to recognise your abilities. Your value is not measured by what you have, who you know, or your background. Your value is based on how God sees you and your understanding of your purpose. Never allow your experiences, or other people's opinions of you, to reduce the value that God has put on you. Everybody is created with value; nobody is without any value. There is something good in and about everybody, everybody has something to offer the world, and everybody can be a blessing. Everything God has ever made has got value; there is nothing God made that has no value. In addition, God made everything for a purpose. You have a purpose, and you were born for an assignment. There is something significant about you that informed your creation.

You are a creative being, endowed with wisdom, great skill, and gifts that the world is seeking. You are anointed, you are an achiever, you can achieve great things, you can climb to that height you dream of, and you can reach that goal. You are a miracle to your generation, you are one of a kind, no one like you exists, and there can never be any one exactly like you. Not only must you see yourself in the correct light, you must also see other people differently, not limiting them by where they are today and not defining their destiny based on the blunders they have made. Never be judgemental; people change and the future for everyone can be different and better. We are all capable of being judgemental and negative in some way. We need to choose to allow God to have His way in our hearts completely, to help us love others the way He does.

You can never have a healthy relationship with anybody being a judgemental and negative person. A negative person can easily turn the pleasantness in a place sour through his negative comments and feedback. When you are always like that, you will notice that people will form an opinion and an attitude towards you. Before you open your mouth to speak, they will already have concluded what you will say. A person is judgemental when he cannot be patient and considerate with the weaknesses of others.

It is important to make clear that there is a difference between making correction and judging people. Corrections show people what they do right and where they get it wrong, whilst also showing them how they can do things better next time. This process can be painful, depending on who you are dealing with. It is understandable that some people don't like being corrected. However, you are being judgemental when your words only put them down and convey the wrong in people, when you don't inspire or encourage others in any way to be better people. People will always feel free to share just anything with you if they know you think highly of them and are ready to support them.

Show People that They Count and Are Important

You must try to make everyone who comes around you feel great. Treat them as if they are special and important to you; show them that you enjoy being with them and working with them. Always see their worth, see the grace of God upon them, and focus on their abilities and not their weaknesses, their contributions and not their failings. See them as very relevant, and treat them as such. When you treat people as inferior, you will not get the best out of them. Never treat anybody as though they are irrelevant. Never treat anybody like they are the only ones who can benefit from the relationship. Never treat anybody like they don't really matter to you and you can do without them. Never treat anybody as though they are a burden or a problem that needs to be sorted out.

When you treat people as rubbish, you don't get the best out of them. You show that you value people when you express to them that you need them, like they too have something to offer you. Also, you show how you value people by the way you speak to them. No matter who the individual is, no matter their achievements or qualifications (or lack thereof), learn to speak to people with respect, like you care about them and recognise they have value to you. In order to show people that they count, you must also learn how to make peace when the relationship is disintegrating. You must be somebody who is easily entreated and who can go all the way to gain back trust, friendship, and loyalty, and no matter how deeply you are hurt, remember to never pay evil for evil.

The value you place on people will always be reflected in how you respond to their infirmity; by this I mean how you relate to them when they are getting it wrong. As a general rule, people will always treat you with respect when you treat them like they are important. They will want to connect with you when you are kind, tolerant, and patient with them. Your good will is always attractive to others.

Never Forget the People Who Have Been Part of Your Story

You demonstrate your value for people and relationship when you don't forget good turns. You show you are not an opportunist and a user of people when you always come back to say thank you for every little help you receive. The fact is that nobody ever achieves anything alone, without an input from someone else. There is much truth in the saying that no man is an island. We all have been taught something by somebody, shown the way of something by somebody, been inspired in some way by somebody, been helped and supported at one point by somebody.

All the people we come into contact with have impacted on our lives in some shape or form. It should be our principle to never forget the good people in our lives and any act of kindness shown to us. We should remember to acknowledge the people who are part of our journey and who have contributed anything into making us who we are today. Never forget the little advice, the little help, the little gift, the little kindness, and the favours that people have granted to you.

> *"And as he entered into a certain village, there met him ten men that were lepers, which stood afar off: And they lifted up their voices, and said, Jesus, Master, have mercy on us. And when he saw them, he said unto them, Go shew yourselves unto the priests. And it came to pass, that, as they went, they were cleansed. And one of them, when he saw that he was healed, turned back, and with a loud voice glorified God, And fell down on his face at his feet, giving him thanks: and he was a Samaritan. And Jesus answering said, were there not ten cleansed? but where are the nine? There are not found that returned to give glory to God, save this stranger. And he said unto him, Arise, go thy way: thy faith hath made thee whole"* (**Luke 17:12-19**).

Never forget the contributions that people have made in your life that have resulted in you becoming the person you are today. Thank God for them, thank them when you can, bless them when you can, and always pray for them. I struggle to understand how some people can forget the people who have contributed to their lives, stood by them and helped them; in some cases, they go as far as treating them as enemies. I struggle to comprehend how you can move on, now that you have become very successful, and treat the people who stood with you when you were nothing as not in your league. I believe this is why God says he hates divorce or putting away; he calls it treachery.

> *"Yet ye say, Wherefore? Because the Lord hath been witness between thee and the wife of thy youth, against whom thou hast dealt treacherously: yet is she thy companion, and the wife of thy covenant. For the Lord, the God of Israel, saith that he hateth putting away: for one covereth violence with his garment, saith the Lord of hosts: therefore take heed to your spirit, that ye deal not treacherously"* (**Malachi 2:14, 16**).

It is treachery to see someone as a misfit and walk away from them when they have been a part of your life, a reason for your achievements. Never forget the person who paid your way through college, never forget the person who was there for you when everybody thought you will never make it, never forget the person who helped you to get to where you are in life. Life is like a seed; you receive back what you do to others. And one good turn deserves another. People who have sown into your life should also have the privilege of partaking in your joy and increase.

The Journey to a Healthy Relationship

Now understand that a healthy relationship does not come about out of the blue; we have to work for it. For a healthy, mature, and fruitful relationship to develop, we need to put the core values of the relationship in view. Using the word "relationship" as an acronym, I would like to explain some of the values I believe make a fruitful and healthy relationship.

R: Reaching out to others

Relationship is about reaching out. You must learn to reach out freely and without any inhibition. The Bible says, "A man that hath friends must show himself friendly: and a friend sticketh closer than a brother" (**Proverbs 18:24**). You must learn to be accommodating to people and tolerant, irrespective of their experiences in life or your differences. You will never be the same with everybody you have to relate with, and a relationship is more beautiful when we are different and are free to express our difference. Relationships are boring when we are all the same.

We must not be afraid to be different, but we must all be accommodative of people and willing to reach out and connect with them, irrespective of who they are. Reaching out involves making a conscious effort to be in constant contact with people in our lives; it involves our willingness to be a part of what is happening to the person. To say that you have reached out to somebody means that the person is able to feel the impact of your love and friendship; something must have left you to deposit in him.

E: Enjoying each other

To make a good relationship, you have to cultivate the joy of seeing and being with the person, even if there are things about them that put you off. It is not everybody you can spend time with, but you have to be willing to spend a lot of time with the people you treasure. You have to learn to deal with every irritation and learn to love them, enjoy their company, and connect with something in them that makes you tick.

Your friendship cannot mature, and you cannot get the best of it, if you are only putting up with him. Until you establish the joy of being around that person, you cannot get the best out of that relationship. The people in your life cannot be free, comfortable, and at the point they can bring out the best in them when they can feel that you are only being long suffering with them. People can feel when you don't enjoy their company and are only bearing with them. If you can genuinely love them, accept them, and see that they are relevant in your life, you will start to find pleasure in them.

L: Loyal to each other

Loyalty is really rare these days. A lot of people are in relationships for conveniences. They ride along when the ride is good, smooth, and easy going. When it becomes rough and turbulent, they jump off the boat and leave you to sink alone. However, loyalty is what makes relationships genuine, healthy, strong, productive, and enduring. You can know that the person in your life is truly a friend and is someone who will never harm you, only if they are loyal to you.

To me, to be loyal means to be faithful and devoted to your friend. You have to be able to defend your friend before his critics and not be a party to anything that will hurt him. You cannot join with others to bad mouth or destroy him and still enjoy a fruitful relationship with him. To be loyal also means to be ready and willing to stand with him, even when things are not going so well with him. The relationship that existed between David and Jonathan, as recorded in **1 Samuel 20:1-42**, is a classic example of what loyalty should look like amongst friends.

A: Available to each other

Being available goes deeper than just living under the same roof with somebody. You can be in the same room with somebody and still be unreachable. You can appear to be in a conversation with somebody and still not be there with him. To be available means the people can access you. It means you are at a place where he can reach out to you. It means to be on hand to provide help and support where there is the need to. It also means to be open and transparent.

Never be at a place where you become so busy that the people you care the most for become second to your job. Never become so important that the people who were once precious to you become less important and can't access you. To make a healthy relationship, people in your life must feel that you care and will be there for them. You need to be there for people when they need you the most. Remember that "a friend in need is a friend indeed."

T: Trusting each other

Some people say, "Never trust anybody." Well, any relationship that is void of trust is insecure and unsafe. Imagine going into a marriage with somebody you cannot trust; imagine what kind of home you are going to have. Imagine surrounding yourself with people you have no trust for; how can you commit to them what is dear to you? How can you go to sleep and be at peace, not knowing whether they will serve your interest or harm you?

Any relationship without trust is bondage. You are going to live in fear, worry, and uncertainty. You are going to be over-suspicious in your dealings, you will be over-protective, and you will lead a destructive life. It's really a pain to relate with people and not trust them. Your ability to trust people releases them to be themselves; it develops in them the confidence to be their best. Your ability to trust frees you from fear. It enables you to make the right investment in people.

To build trust in a relationship, you will need to learn how not to base your opinions of your friend on what you hear others say of him. Learn to believe in him even when you have your doubts. Your relationship ought to be based on the love of God. The Bible says, "Love believes all things." Learn to doubt your doubt and believe. When people say that you believe in them, they do their best not to fail you. Another scripture says, "Perfect love cast out fear." As love for people matures in you, you will notice that trust for them grows also. As trust grows, fear vanishes, unnecessary worry fades away.

I: Interested in each other

Your spouse, your friends, your employees or employer, and everyone you have a relationship with will like to know that you are interested in them. The person wants to know that you are not in the relationship for the sex, the money, the name, and whatever benefit there is in the relationship. If your spouse thinks that you are only interested in the sex, the sex becomes tasking. If it's about the material benefits, then he or she becomes less enthusiastic about you too. Your employees will put in their best when they can see that you are not only on and about the profit but their well-being too. Likewise your employer, he will keep you, can trust you with more, and will invest in you if he knows that you care about his interest.

People naturally commit more, give more, make sacrifices to make it work when they can see that interest is shown in them. You show you are interested in somebody by how well you know him or your interest to know more about him as a person. It is important to know about his career, hobbies, friends, and other areas of his interest. You need to get interested in what makes him happy and try to contribute what you can to make him succeed. You need to start to listen more, pay more attention, and get more involved in what concerns him.

O: Obedient to God with each other

As a believer, you really need to be aware of the people you are assigned to and also know the role you are to play in their lives and engage it in obedience to God, no matter what. Sometimes, you are going to have to bless people not because you think they deserve it but because that is what God is saying you must do. You also need to know the person's worth, gifts, and what value he brings and in obedience to God create the room for him to excel in it. If we are obedient to God with each other, we are not going to be threatened by the gift and the ability in the other person, we are not going to stand in the way of the other person, we are not going to defraud each other, we are not going to abuse or take advantage of each other, we are not going to hold back but release what we need to that will help the other person to succeed, and no matter what happens, we will not break, separate, or divorce.

In obedience to God with each other, it also means that you do not compromise your standing with God because of any relationship; remember that God must always come first. In your obedience to God, help the person to know what God is saying about them and what you can do to help them achieve it. Show the person what God is showing you and show him what God has taught you. Don't withhold anything good that you know can make him into a better person.

N: Needing each other

You must be conscious of the fact that God will not bring anybody into your life unless they are relevant to your destiny. You really need the people who are in your life to achieve your purpose here on earth. Never assume the position that you can do without anybody; you really need people. Remember I said earlier, there is something that you may never have until someone gives it to you. There is a place you may never go to until someone takes you there. There is something you may never know until someone shows you. There are people you need to meet but may never get to meet them until someone introduces you to them. We all need the people who are in our lives. And they need to know that they are relevant and that we need them.

You must never forget that you and your friend are both vital in God's plan for each other and that you need each other to fulfil your purpose here on the earth. Don't treat anybody you are in a relationship with like they need you the most or as though you can do without them. People will not commit and will easily walk away for the slightest reason when they can sense that you don't need them. Learn to freely show people how important they are to you; it does not make you less a man in any way. Show them how much you value every little help they give you, never taking them or anything for granted. Never treat a friend like he is not relevant; never treat a friend like he is a pest or a burden, not even when he makes little or no contribution today. You never can tell, tomorrow might be different; situations really change in life. One of the ways that you show somebody that they are important to you is still standing by them and not walking away when they make a blunder.

S: Supporting each other

Relationship is healthy and is more beautiful when the people in it are not more about what they can gain from each other but what they can bring to help make the other person become the best he can be. We all have something to give; there is something we can all do to inspire or give a boost to the other person. Don't only look out for your own need; learn to look out for what you can do to make your friend more successful and more comfortable. Be a supportive friend. Be financially, spiritually, emotionally, and materially committed to each other. Do not just love in words, learn to give. Be there for your friend when he is in need. "It is more blessed to give than to receive" should be one of the guiding principles in your relationship.

Also you need to be mindful that your friend will sometimes make a blunder in life. When that happens, don't be a fault finder, a negative and condemning person. When your friend has made a mess of things, don't make him feel more worthless and helpless. When he is weak and in need is the time he needs your support the most. It's sad that that is the time a lot of friends walk away. Your friend needs your support when he is down. Support him to pick up the pieces, regain his confidence, and try again. Don't let people in your life fight their battles alone; support them in their fight. Assure them of your love and support. When people in your life go down, don't let them stay down, help them rise. When people in your life are in trouble, see what needs to be done to resolve it. The Bible says, "Brethren, if a man be overtaken in a fault, ye which are spiritual, restore such an one in the spirit of meekness; considering thyself, lest thou also be tempted" (**Galatians 6:1**).

H: Helping each other

By helping each other, I mean to assist in any way possible, to lend a hand to a friend to do their work, to help to speed up the process or to reduce the burden. Nobody should be in a good relationship and be seen to be carrying his burden alone, like he has got nobody in his life. The Bible says, "Bear ye one another's burdens, and so fulfil the law of Christ" (**Galatians 6:2**). Get involved in your friend's life; don't let them do things alone, especially when you can do something to lighten the burden or speed up the process.

You can help with their work, domestic, career, or academic, wherever you can. You can help with the house chores when you are there. You can help with gardening when they are too busy or ill. You can help with the school run. You can help clear the bills when it becomes a pain. You can help with picking up the groceries. You can help to bring out the bin. If you look well, you will see that there is always something you can do to make life comfortable for your friend. Always give a helping hand to reduce the burden and to help your friend achieve the best. You can be a part of your friend's success story, by being there for them and helping them in the small things as well as the large things. When you help, you increase your worth in the person's heart, and you strengthen what you've got together.

I: Investing in each other

What really makes a relationship beautiful is what everyone brings into it to make the other person a better person. Relationships are healthy and more rewarding if everyone's first passion is put on what they can contribute than what they can get out of it. You have to be willing to invest in the people who are in your life to achieve success in a relationship.

Your willingness to invest in something demonstrates the value you put on it. Your willingness to invest shows you believe in the future of the thing; you show that something better can come of it. To achieve a fruitful relationship requires that you invest your time, faith, resources, and whatever the relationship requires. Never hold back what you know, if released, can help to transform the other person. Your investment is the only thing that can empower the people in your life. When they are empowered, they succeed in life. When they succeed, you will enjoy the dividend. You will always have a good return from a good investment.

P: Praying for and with each other

It is said that the family that prays together, stays together. This is actually a true saying. When you start to pray for people, even when you don't particularly like them, with time you will discover that you will start to develop love for them. When you start to meet and pray with somebody, though you may be having relational challenges with him, over time you will start to notice that the little problems are fading away. Prayer has a way of bringing and bonding people together. You will always, over time, in the place of prayer, develop love and passion for the thing you are praying for. So if you desire a fruitful relationship with anybody, explore prayer; it really works. In the place of prayer, the Holy Spirit will work in you and in the situation you are praying for and will bring something beautiful as a result.

Sometimes, a relationship becomes difficult because of our individual problems we bring into it. This is why you need to keep your friend's needs and concerns in your prayers. The best thing you can give to a friend is your time spent in prayer for him. Your prayers can go a long way to helping to provide protection around him, favour wherever he goes and wisdom in the area of his assignment. Everybody, no matter who they are, is in need of a prayer support. Sometimes, our relationships become difficult as a result of an attack from our enemy Satan. In prayer, we are able to contend and overcome all the attacks of the enemy against us. Prayer helps to bring God into the situation. Don't ignore the place of prayer; it helps to keep families together.

S: Strengthening each other

There is a time that you must be strong for the sake of somebody. You will need to be strong so you can be a pillar and succour to him. There will be a time that it is only when you are strong that your friend can pull through and survive it. When his faith is weak, and he is offended in God, he will need you to stand. When there is bereavement and he is feeling hopeless, he will need you to stand. When it is tough for him at work and he feels like quitting, he needs you to strengthen him to stay the course. When he feels rejected and it's like everyone else does not understand him, he will need you to provide him assurance.

Even Jesus at some point in His life needed strengthening. For the Bible says:

> "And he was withdrawn from them about a stone's cast, and kneeled down, and prayed, Saying, Father, if thou be willing, remove this cup from me: nevertheless not my will, but thine, be done. And there appeared an angel unto him from heaven, strengthening him. And being in an agony he prayed more earnestly: and his sweat was as it were great drops of blood falling down to the ground" (**Luke 22:41-44**).

As a friend, you must be a source of inspiration and encouragement, especially in the things of God to your friends. Take every opportunity to help your friend to grow in his relationship with God. Encourage him in the area of prayer and in the need for him to attain believers' fellowship. Never be the reason why your friend won't love Jesus. Your friend needs you when he is down. Your friend needs you when he is unemployed and broke. Your friend needs you when he is going through separation or divorce. Your friend needs you to help strengthen him when things become tough and he is about to give up. Your friend needs you to understand and not judge him when he has made that blunder and everything seems to be crashing down on him. Your friend needs you to be a source of strength to him. The Bible says, "Iron sharpened iron; so a man sharpeneth the countenance of his friend" (**Proverbs 27:17**). You must be that iron in your friend's life.

Understand the Place of a Spiritual Father

> "For though ye have ten thousand instructers in Christ, yet have ye not many fathers: for in Christ Jesus I have begotten you through the gospel. Wherefore I beseech you, be ye followers of me. For this cause have I sent unto you Timotheus, who is my beloved son, and faithful in the Lord, who shall bring you into remembrance of my

ways which be in Christ, as I teach everywhere in every church" **(1 Corinthians 4:15-17)**.

Everybody, especially a believer, needs a spiritual father. Somebody he can learn from, somebody he can look up to, somebody he is submitted to, somebody who can call him to order and make him do things that he may not do by himself. A spiritual father is somebody who has already gone down the road you want to go down. He has been through and seen what you have not experienced. A spiritual father is a mentor, a coach, and a guide in the ways of the kingdom. I have seen that some young people, after one experience of anointing, think that they have arrived and no longer need guidance. Just because you lay your hands on somebody and he falls does not mean that you are now an invincible man of God, who does not need anybody teaching and coaching you.

No matter how great we become, we all need somebody who has gone ahead of us, somebody who by experience has discovered what we don't know yet. We all need somebody we can be accountable to and learn from. It is sad that you can see people starting out in Christian ministry, even planting churches, and yet do not have a mentor or a father figure in their lives that they are accountable to. It is a travesty to think that you are capable of teaching and mentoring others when you are not accountable to anyone yourself; you need to lead by example, this includes being accountable to a mentor or spiritual father. If you want to go far in life, if you want to stay within certain boundaries, you need a father. You need somebody you can submit to. We all need a father.

A father is much more than just a teacher. Paul the apostle wrote to the church in Corinth, *"Even though you have ten thousand guardians in Christ, you do not have many fathers, for in Christ Jesus I became your father through the gospel"* (**1 Corinthians 4:15,** NIV). It is okay to have other people whose teaching, grace, and anointing you value, and you allow them to speak into your life. However, a father's voice must sound louder than any other voice in your life; a father must have a place in your heart that they do not occupy. His teachings and his interpretations must have a higher value than what others teach such that you interpret all teaching in the light of the Bible and what he has said.

A father is the one you are following first under Christ and is somebody you will never be able to say no to, argue with, or play the "I know it too" game with. Before a father, you are always the receiver, especially in the matters of the spirit, no matter what you know. A father is somebody you learn from, not somebody you want to try to teach. A father is somebody whose word is authority in your life; he is somebody you always listen to. He is the one person you can trust to instruct you appropriately, the one who can call you to order when you are missing the mark. You can't call a father to order; you can't rebuke him. You may not be always happy with him, but by virtue of his position in your life, you can't rebuke him.

The problem with a lot of young people today is that they don't want anybody telling them what to do. They think they know more than everybody. Many people, especially the young, but not exclusively the young, don't want anybody giving them permission or the go-ahead before they do something. They think that as far as what they want to embark on is from heaven, then that is it. But you see, it takes time to build muscles, spiritual muscles. It takes some time of spiritual exercises to really discern the ways of the Spirit. I have dealt with young people who have come up with certain ideas, some of them about marriage, and insisted it was God who was leading them into it; however, after a little while, they come to see me again to say, "It is not working; I think I got it wrong."

We all have the tendency to get it wrong, but we can save ourselves from a lot of trouble if we can put ourselves in a place where we can be accountable to the right person. A father is somebody you can trust to provide you with a covering and take responsibility for you. You expect a father to defend you and speak for you when there is the need. You want him to be there for you when it is good and when it is challenging. It really can become rough and challenging in the journey of life, and sometimes things become difficult for us as a result of our own failings or blunders. At such times, we need support; we need people standing by us to pray and help us rise up again so we can keep moving.

We need somebody who cares, who has our best interests at heart, helping us to break through. I have seen many people fall and not get up because they had no one they listened to. A father is somebody you should trust with your struggles and battles. He must be somebody you are not ashamed to share your inner fights with, because you know he will only want to help you out. He must be somebody you can run to for help, somebody you can count on to pray with you and for you.

A father is somebody who can provide you with guidance and leadership. He shows you how to do it by example. You are inspired by his achievements and character. If you cannot follow his example or copy him in his style, then he cannot be a spiritual father. He must be somebody you admire and want to learn from. **Proverbs 4:1** says, *"Hear ye children, the instruction of a father, and attend to know understanding."* He must be your man of wisdom even if you are witnessing more results in your work in comparison to his. He must be somebody you can trust to help discern, interpret, confirm, or affirm your dreams, visions, and calling.

I have found that many people like to call somebody "Father," but the moment you start to instruct them in a way they are not happy with, they don't remember that you are their father any more. You are not going to be able to get it right if all you want to be told is what you want to hear. The role of a father is to say it as it is and support you to make the tough decisions. As such, he should also stand by you to defend you where it all goes wrong. A father is also your introducer. He is somebody who likes to help you expand and enlarge. He desires to see you succeed, so he finds ways to introduce you to people, things, and places that can benefit you. Ultimately, he serves as a destiny helper in your life.

Honouring a Father

A father is somebody who deserves your honour. Malachi writes, *"A son honoureth his father, and a servant his master: if then I be a father, where is mine honour? And if I be a master, where is my fear? Saith the Lord of hosts unto you, O priests, that despise my name. And ye say wherein we have despised thy name"* (**Malachi 1:6**). To "honour" could mean a few things, but it includes respecting somebody by taking his word seriously and doing what he says. The opposite of honour is to despise. You despise somebody when his word means nothing to you, when you don't care how he feels about a thing and you don't want to know. It therefore shows honour to any man when you regard his words as having authority over you.

Another way the Bible shows us to honour a father is with our substance. You cannot say you are honouring a father and not be a blessing to him in carnal things. You demonstrate honour by giving to a father. You don't give to a father because he's got a need; you give to show you value him. Another way to honour a father is by having regular contact. Don't stay away until you need help to get out of trouble or you have a need to be met. You honour a father when you maintain contact; you want him to know from time to time how things are going with you as well as calling just to check on him.

CHAPTER 4

Single, Married, Not Alone

"An unmarried man is concerned about the Lord's affairs, how he can please the Lord. But a married man is concerned about the affairs of this world, how he can please his wife, and his interests are divided. An unmarried woman [or girl] is concerned about the Lord's affairs: Her aim is to be devoted to the Lord in both body and spirit. But a married woman is concerned about the affairs of this world, how she can please her husband" (**1 Corinthians 7:32-34, NIV**).

I would like to emphasise that there is nothing wrong with not being married. It is not wrong to stay single. Never think that because you are not yet married and are of marriageable age, you are in sin, you are under a curse or you have an abnormal life. There is nothing wrong or abnormal about being single. Actually, it is God's own design that some people should stay unmarried. Consider these scriptures:

"The disciples said to him, 'If this is the situation between a husband and wife, it is better not to marry.' Jesus replied, 'Not everyone can accept this word, but only those to whom it has been given. For some are eunuchs because they were born that way; others were made that way by men; and others have renounced marriage

because of the kingdom of heaven. The one who can accept this should accept it'" (**Matthew 19:10-12, NIV**).

"I wish everyone could get along without marrying, just as I do. But we are not all the same. God gives some the gift of a husband or wife, and others he gives the gift of being able to stay happily unmarried. So I say to those who aren't married and to widows: better to stay unmarried if you can, just as I am" (**1 Corinthians 7:7-8, TLB**).

As you can see, the Bible says that you can be more devoted and more available to be used of God by being single than being married. It says in **1 Corinthians 7:32-34 (NIV),** *"An unmarried man is concerned about the Lord's affairs, how he can please the Lord. But a married man is concerned about the affairs of this world, how he can please his wife, and his interests are divided. An unmarried woman [or girl] is concerned about the Lord's affairs: Her aim is to be devoted to the Lord in both body and spirit. But a married woman is concerned about the affairs of this world, how she can please her husband."* There are many great men in the Bible that never married.

For instance, Jesus Christ, Paul the apostle, and John the Baptist were never married. They did not marry, yet they achieved great things, and we never heard that they were lonely or depressed. If you are single, don't allow that to make you feel you are at a disadvantage in any way, because you are not. Don't allow being single to make you feel as though you have got a problem. Don't allow being single to make you feel like you are less than others; you are not less in any way, shape, or form. Therefore, enjoy being you, just as you are; maximise every moment of your life and live life to the full. Don't let the devil steal your joy; the plan of God for your life is different from that of everyone else.

There is a difference between being single and being alone. That you are not married should not make you lonely. If you cannot develop and enjoy quality relationships with people of both sexes while single, you are likely going to be a miserable wife or husband. You can and should enjoy a quality life and not live in loneliness as a single person. However, it is all up to you to do this. You can choose to get many things going for you, like devoting yourself to your work or studies, or enjoying and engaging in serving God in your church. Most importantly, you need to engage with people; you need to pay attention to people. Be a people person, be friendly, be sociable and approachable. Do not be the hard-to-get type; it does not make you cheap when you are approachable. You are cheap only if you allow yourself to go to bed with somebody you are not married to, somebody who just wants to see your underwear. Ladies, you are not that cheap, are you?

Blessed, Satisfied, and Complete

You need to settle in the truth that you are blessed and must find happiness and fulfilment just as you are. For in Christ Jesus, you are complete (see **Colossians 2:10**). Whether there is a man or woman in your life or not, you should find joy in living, serving, and just being who you are. Marriage is good, empowering, and commendable, but that does not mean that without marriage you are not complete, or that you cannot be fulfilled, or that you cannot reach your goal.

A good marriage is about two complete and encouraged people coming together to complement each other. When one of the parties in marriage is half-baked, too dependent, uninspired, dependency will be one sided and there will be a lot of strain in the marriage; the marriage will suffer. For the Bible says in **Proverbs 27:17 (NIV)**, *"As iron sharpens iron, so one man sharpens another."* It is iron that sharpens iron; wood cannot sharpen iron. Both the man and the woman have got to be iron to make a good marriage.

As a single person who desires marriage, do not just put all your energy into finding the right person, who has all the right qualities that you are seeking in a partner. You also need to spend time learning to be the right person, the quality you, the inspired you, the fulfilled you. It is a tragedy if you are tying your happiness in life to another person. If you are happy by yourself, and fulfilled and inspired as a person, you are most likely going to bring that into your marriage. If you don't feel complete by yourself, then you are not ready for marriage.

So You Think You Are Up for Marriage?

Okay, you want to get married, right? Marriage is a good thing. But is it for you? Are you ready for marriage? I am of the opinion that until you are starting to really think about marriage, you should not get into any serious relationship. Don't tell anybody, "I love you" or "I want to be with you." It is okay to be good friends with somebody of the opposite sex; I think everybody should strive to make friends of both sexes. It is okay to go out together for dinner or even go to watch a movie, not necessarily because there is an intention for anything serious to develop between you two; it is that you are just being friends and you both know it. But never say, "I love you," until you mean it. In addition, don't enter into marriage simply because everyone around you is married or because of pressure put on you by society or your family.

If you want to get married, you should do so because you understand what marriage is for, you know that you are ready for it and have found God's will for your life. That person must believe that together with the other person, they are going to find companionship, will serve God better, and can bring joy and happiness into each other's life. Until you are ready and prepared for marriage, do not go into it. If you do enter marriage prematurely, you are highly likely to cause pain to the person you are married to. Also, you know you are ready for marriage when you are mentally mature. In other words, you have learned how to treat your spouse with respect. You have trained yourself in the acts of loving, caring, and sharing.

Paul the apostle writes, *"When I was a child, I spake as a child, I understood as a child, I thought as a child; but when I became a man, I put away childish things"* (**1 Corinthians 13:11**). There is growing up to do before marriage, because God, who designed it, intended for it to be between grownups and not children. You also know you are ready for marriage when you are settled in a career or ministry. You are not yet ready if you have no direction in life. You are not ready to start a family if you are not yet able to support a family. No man should bring home any man's daughter by faith, and no man should marry a woman because he thinks she can take care of the family. There is a need to grow up in many areas, if that is the line of your thinking. The Bible says:

> *"But if any provide not for his own, and especially for those of his own house, he hath denied the faith, and is worse than an infidel"* (**1 Timothy 5:8**).

When Your Season Comes, God Makes All Things Beautiful

As a child of God, you need to know that if marriage is in God's plan for you, God will in His time be faithful to bring somebody into your life, somebody you can develop a relationship with. You may start off as just friends, but it may lead to marriage. From experience, I have found that it is better marrying somebody who started out as a friend; actually, marriage between two friends is usually very successful. For any marriage to work, the man and the woman in the marriage must exist as friends.

Friendship is the highest form of relationship, which is why Abraham is called the friend of God. Moreover, at one point in His relationship with His disciples, Jesus said unto them (in **John 15:15**), *"Henceforth I call you not servants; for the servant knoweth not what his lord doeth: but I have called you friends; for all things that I have heard of my Father I have made known unto you."* The Bible says also in **Proverbs 18:24,** *"A man that hath friends must shew himself friendly: and there is a friend that sticketh closer than* *a brother."* It is of utmost importance that you make yourself friendly if you really want to keep people in your life, and you should choose your friends carefully, as you never can tell where that friendship will lead to.

Now the point I am trying to make is that if marriage is in the plan of God for you, He is faithful, and at some point in your life, He is going to bring you into contact with people He wants you to form relationships with. To get it right, it is important that you do not take for granted or despise anybody that God brings into your life. The person may not appear right today, but God has a plan. The person may not be coming from where you expect your marriage partner to come from, but never limit God. The person may not be somebody important today, but people change; the person you look down on today may become somebody more powerful than you can imagine.

Michelle Obama never knew that the man she turned down a few times before she eventually said yes and agreed to marry was going to become the forty-fourth president of the United States of America. Learn to show humility; be approachable and friendly to all the people God is surrounding you with. If we desire friendship, the Bible has urged us to show ourselves friendly to those around us. You are only going to push people away if you despise them or are not friendly. In some cases, the people you are going to push away are likely to be the people who matter in your destiny, the people God is seeking to link you with because of what the future holds.

If you ask ladies who are of marriageable age, still single, and waiting for the right man, you may discover that for a strong proportion of them, it was not that nobody in the past showed any interest in them: you will discover that at some point in their lives, they were either not sensitive enough to the timing of God or at the time the men were approaching, they did not want any relationship. They thought they were not ready, they were solely focused on achieving education or career development. As such, they failed to make themselves friendly, and it passed them by.

Others might likely be those who also had men show an interest but did not think the guys fitted in with their criteria; to them, these men were not tall enough, not educated enough, not in the right profession, not from the tribe, nation, or colour they desired them to come from, and so on. They did not fit in, and it passed them by. (Still others may have hung onto the wrong guy in the hope that he would become marriage material, so no other man would approach as she gave the impression that she was taken.)

Never forget, God is faithful, and He will bring the people who matter in your destiny across your path, but it is for you to allow some things to happen. Ladies and gentlemen, don't base your decision on what the other person has achieved in life. Marriage is one of the most important decisions in your life; therefore, it requires prayer and serious thought. As marriage is a big thing, there is no way you are going to be able to hear God regarding it when you cannot hear God in little things, like when to go on a fast, when to make a sacrifice or sow a seed of faith, or when to pray for somebody. If you are ready to start a serious relationship which will lead to marriage, here are some useful tips that can help you to make the right choice.

If You Don't Pray about It, You Have No Way of Knowing what God Says about It

To connect with the right person, firstly it is very important that you take time to pray and, if possible, fast and seek God's face about it. The Bible in **Proverbs 3:5-6** says, *"Trust in the Lord with all thine heart; and lean not unto thine own understanding. In all thy ways acknowledge him, and he shall direct thy paths."* If you take time to pray about it, God will favour you and will lead you to the right person. Don't just jump into anything without first seeking the face of God concerning it. It also says in **Proverbs 14:12**, *"There is a way that seemeth right unto a man, but the end thereof are the ways of death,"* and **Isaiah 48:17** says, *"Thus saith the Lord, thy redeemer, the Holy one of Israel; I am the Lord thy*

God, which teacheth thee to profit, which leadeth thee by the way that thou shouldest go."

Secondly, you must look out for the fear of God in the person you are considering. God will be faithful and bring somebody into your life you can develop some sort of relationship with. However, you ought to know that God will not lead you to marry somebody who has no regard for Him. Thirdly, you also want to ask yourself how much you love the person and what kind of love it is. Love is the pillar of any good relationship. It is love that sustains relationships through challenging times. In reality, every marriage will face challenges, but as the Bible says, "Many waters cannot quench love" (**Song of Solomon 8:7**). In challenging times, it is the love that you share that will form the rock on which you stand.

God will not lead you to marry somebody you do not love. He only gives us what we appreciate. So never say, "I don't love this person but will still go ahead and marry him because I am obeying God." To make a good marriage, two kinds of love are required: the first is **agape,** and that is the God kind of love, or unconditional love. The God kind of love is inherent only in believers of Christ. It is love that makes you selfless, the love that can enable you to lay down anything for the person, the love that can enable you to forgive anything, the love that never judges. Without agape, your marriage will not last. The second kind of love is **Eros**. Eros is sexual attraction. You need Eros as well to enjoy a great and lasting marriage.

Never say, "I want to marry this person, even though I don't fancy him; I don't really like her figure, she is not my type." I have heard people say, "Don't look for beauty, look for character." No, you need to look out for both. You need to find the person who is sexually and physically attractive to you. She must look beautiful in your eyes, and he must look handsome in your eyes. If you don't keep physical beauty in mind in your decision making, tomorrow you are going to compare the person with someone else and wish you had married them instead. You are going to wake up someday and wonder what the person lying by your side is doing there. Don't only see the person in the spirit; you are not going to live with a spirit but a human being, and you are not going to live in the spirit with the person, but in the real world. Get real, open your eyes wide, and look very carefully to make sure that what you can see is precious to you. Hear these scriptures from the Song of Solomon:

> "Make this promise, O women of Jerusalem—If you find my lover, tell him I am weak with love. Young Women of Jerusalem. Why is your lover better than all others, O woman of rare beauty? What makes your lover so special that we must promise this? Young Woman My lover is dark and dazzling, better than ten thousand others! His head is finest gold, his wavy hair is black as a raven. His eyes sparkle like doves beside springs of water; they are set like jewels washed in milk. His cheeks are like gardens of spices giving off fragrance. His lips are like lilies, perfumed with myrrh. His arms are like rounded bars of gold, set with beryl. His body is like bright ivory, glowing with lapis lazuli. His legs are like marble pillars set in sockets of finest gold. His posture is stately, like the noble cedars of Lebanon. His mouth is sweetness itself; he is desirable in every way. Such, O women of Jerusalem, is my lover, my friend" (**Song of Solomon 5:8-16, NLT**).

> "Let your wife be a fountain of blessing for you. Rejoice in the wife of your youth. She is a loving deer, a graceful doe. Let her breasts satisfy you always. May you always be captivated by her love" (**Proverbs 5:18-19, NLT**).

Perhaps you never thought verses like this would be found in the Bible; they certainly are, and so many more like them. God put them there because He is interested in us having a deep passion for our lovers, and it gives Him pleasure when we can behold our spouses and admire the beautiful things He has deposited in them.

Beware of Time Wasters, They Interrupt God's Plan

Before you commit to anybody, you need to ask about their plan and vision in life. You need to know what their plan is for their life and find out when they intend to marry. I like goal-oriented relationships, relationships that got started with the due date for marriage in mind; that is why I say to young people, until you start to think about marriage, don't say, "I love you and would like to marry you someday."

You need to have the understanding of when the "someday" would be. This is to ladies especially: if you are going into a serious relationship with a man, it is important for you to really know what his plans for marriage are and ensure those plans are in line with yours. For example, don't commit to anybody as a husband-to-be, until you are sure that he is not just talking about being friends or wants to try things out first and see what happens. His intentions about the relationship must be made clear from day one. Otherwise, he can walk away three, four, five years later after wasting your time. Remember, you are not growing any younger as the days go by.

I can tell you confidently that this is one of the reasons why some older ladies are still single today. They once got in a relationship with a man who was uncommitted, who held them down for years in an unending relationship, and who eventually left them in limbo. She started with him when she was twenty-six years old and went out with him for five years, but he walked away for some reason, and she is now thirty-one years old and desperate to settle. You really need to understand their season for marriage and check this timing with yours.

Don't Ignore Your Season, Flow with It

For example, say you are twenty-two years old and are hoping to be married in three to four years; if a man who is twenty-three years old asks you out but is still in the university and does not intend to marry for six to seven years, the question is, are you prepared to wait until then? You are going to be twenty-eight to twenty-nine years old by the time he is finally ready; should that be okay with you?

If you want to wait for him, that is good, but do you see him sticking with you for the next seven years? Is he that committed? Will he make good on his promises? In addition, you need to be aware that in most cases, if you are going out with somebody, even if he is not serious about you, nobody else will come to ask you out. You see, as long as you and he are together, God will not send somebody else to you; He is not the author of confusion.

My opinion is that the best thing is to believe that God will send you a man who is ready for marriage when you are ready. A twenty-year-old man like you will only be twenty-three years old in three years' time; most men are not ready for marriage at that age. Although this is not always the case, it is essential for you to be sure you understand what you are going into; otherwise, you are going to be with the man for a good number of years and may have to start courting all over again. What I am trying to say is do not enter into a relationship that might end up being a waste of your time. Any separation at whatever stage has the tendency to hurt you. Remember that as long as you are with somebody, it puts a barrier between you and your true spouse that God intends for you.

He Does Not Deserve You if He has No Respect for You

Check the person's sense of responsibility. If you are faithful to God and you wait on Him, He will not give you an irresponsible person, I mean someone who will not have regard for you and who will treat you like you have no value. **Hebrews 11:6** says, *"But without faith it is impossible to please him: for he that cometh to God must believe that he is, and that he is a rewarder of them that diligently seek him."* God will not connect you with someone who has no regard for your parents, someone who has no purpose or goal in life, someone who will only use you and walk away. God will not give you someone selfish, lazy, or unproductive, someone who will end up being a pain and a burden, someone who is abusive.

If you can see that the person is a busybody and full of talk and no real action, you may need to tell him to first sort himself out, and then he can come to you. Only commit to going out with somebody who shows you respect, who has regard for your parents, who is willing and ready to be the bread winner, who wants to take responsibility for you. However, you must not limit anybody to where he is now. People do change and progress, and only God knows what tomorrow will bring. My own beautiful wife would not have married me if she had considered what I was when we first met; she says it was my person, my character, my dream, and what God told her that attracted her to me. You may also want to look out for the person's attitude to learning, his attitude towards work, and how he deals with people. His vision, his drive, and his fear for God are fundamental things you must not overlook.

You need to also consider your compatibility. No two people are the same, so you are to expect to be different in some ways. Marriage is more exciting if the two of you don't see things the same way and don't do things the same, but you must agree on fundamental issues. For the Bible says in **Amos 3:3,** *"Can two walk together, except they be agreed?"* It also says in **Matthew 12:25,** *"And Jesus knew their thoughts, and said unto them, Every kingdom divided against itself is brought to desolation; and every city or house divided against itself shall not stand."* It is a big problem if you are different on fundamental issues, like your faith, your desire for children, and whether the woman intends to work or be a housewife. If your values are different, then you need to pray some more. If he or she is a match made from heaven, then there will be chemistry. You will agree on the most important things.

Your Relationship with God Is Connected to what He Called You to Do

Consider your spiritual calling, especially if you are a Christian interested in full-time ministry. What you need to fully understand is that your relationship with God is one and the same with His calling for your life. You cannot and should not separate your relationship with God from His purpose for your creation, from how He wants you to live your life, or from what He wants you to do for Him. The quality of your relationship with God is determined by your total obedience to His calling in your life. If you are interested in full-time ministry, then you need to know what the person you want to be with thinks about it.

Don't marry anybody who has no regard for your calling or who is not open to the unexpected from God. It's also true that you may not sense God's calling right now, but He may speak to you regarding that in the future. If the person you are with is saying, "I can never marry a minister," then you need to be careful. I know a man whose wife left him because he said God was calling him into full-time Christian ministry. Before they got married, they had both agreed that they were not going to be involved in any ministry, for she had told him that she did not want to be a minister's wife; when he started leaning towards ministry, she felt betrayed and left him.

It's important to note that the family does not come before Christ; following Christ is superior to the family. You cannot forsake your calling for the sake of your family, because you cannot follow Christ if you are not willing and able to forsake them for Him. Jesus made it clear when He said:

> "And every one that hath forsaken houses, or brethren, or sisters, or father, or mother, or wife, or children, or lands, for my name's sake, shall receive an hundredfold, and shall inherit everlasting life" (**Matthew 19:29**).

However, you don't have to put yourself in a position where you have to choose between God and your loved ones; you need a spouse and a family that will stand by you and support you to fulfil your heavenly vision. And as for marriage, you need to come to an understanding of where both of you stand with regards to your calling. Your decision on whether you are with the right person or not should be based on this understanding.

The Family Is Relevant, Don't Overlook It

You must look at your potential partner's family history. Family history and background do not determine God's purpose in marriage, but you need to know the person's family background and history so you are aware of what you are going into. For instance, it is important to know if there is sickle cell or some other illness in the person's family. This may not affect your decision, but you want to know what you are up against. This knowledge helps you know your battle and better prepares you for the journey.

Also, you need to consider what your parents say about the relationship. Parental consent to a believer must never be disregarded; you need parental consent to go ahead with your marriage, because the Bible teaches, "Honour your father and mother . . . that it may be well with you and you may live long on the earth" (**Ephesians 6:2-3**). Parental consent does not mean that you are to leave it to your parents to make a choice regarding who you are to marry; that is not what I mean. Don't give them that power. They love you and want the best for you, but they are not to make your choice for you.

You do, however, need to listen to their advice and weigh it in the light of what you think is best for you. If your parents disagree with your marriage, don't just go ahead with it and ignore them; remember, you need to honour them. Patiently wait for them and pray until they come round. With some persuasion, you will bring them to realise how much you love the person. You need their blessing. You can help to persuade them by involving a third party they have regard for.

Where There Is Counsel, There Is Safety

You need to seek for counselling in your decision making. **Proverbs 11:14** says, *"Where no counsel is, the people fall: but in the multitude of counselors there is safety,"* and **Proverbs 15:22** also says, *"Without counsel purposes are disappointed: but in the multitude of counselors they are established."* You need assurance that you have got it right, and you can only know that through counselling. Remember that the Bible also says, *"By the mouth of two or three witnesses every word shall be established"* (**2 Corinthians 13:1**). I have seen people end up in trouble because they refused to be counselled before getting married.

It's important to seek counselling from your parents, especially if they are born again; seek counsel from someone who has a parental or mentorship role in your life, but most importantly, seek counselling from your pastor. Never go into a serious relationship without first seeking advice from your pastor; if you don't have a pastor, go and find one. We all need a pastor. God says, *"And I will give you pastors according to mine heart, which shall feed you with knowledge and understanding"* (**Jeremiah 3:15**). Whatever the case, you are the one to make the ultimate decision; counselling should only help you to clarify that decision.

Another useful tip is for you to take time to know each other before you seal the deal. It is most interesting when love develops between two friends; it is okay to fall in love with someone you started out with as a friend. I encourage you to have a period of courtship before marriage; don't just meet somebody and arrange marriage straight away. Marrying someone you know so little about is not a clever thing to do. Someone you intend to live with for the rest of your life should be someone you know quite well. The essence of courtship is not to find out God's will: don't go into courtship until you are sure you have found the right person; otherwise, you are going to be breaking somebody's hopes and expectations. That hurts. Courtship can help you work out your differences and develop friendship and intimacy. It is essentially meant to help you channel the pattern or style your relationship will take. Marriage is meant to be enjoyed; if you don't develop friendship before marriage, you may end up spending the best part of it trying to resolve differences that could have been sorted before marriage.

Dealing with the Stigma of Singleness

If you are mature but still single, you may think there is a curse or demonic embargo on your life. I come from Nigeria, where people tend to relate every event to spiritual factors. We like to relate our situations to our background (usually referred to as generational curses). Another factor is that we also come from backgrounds of polygamy; there is often family jealousy, and we have seen many people wounded by it. As such, people often wonder if this is due to them being under a curse, a spell, or witchcraft. They wonder whether somebody else is responsible for their situation. If you are born again, I would like you to know that you are in freedom. Here is what Paul says:

> "Giving thanks unto the Father, which hath made us meet to be partakers of the inheritance of the saints in light: Who hath delivered us from the power of darkness, and hath translated us into the kingdom of his dear Son. In whom we have redemption through his blood, even the forgiveness of sins" (**Colossians 1:12-14, KJV**).

There are three things in these verses that I would like you to consider. Firstly, it says we have received forgiveness of sins and redemption through the blood of Jesus (by redemption, it means that the penalty for all the implications of your sins are all paid for, and you now no longer have to pay for it). Secondly, it says we are delivered from the kingdom of darkness (we are now citizens of the kingdom of Jesus). Therefore, Satan no longer has authority over us or over our destiny. Thirdly, it says we are now qualified to be partakers of the inheritance of the saints (meaning you qualify to experience the goodness of God). However, until you accept it and start to act like this is who you really are in Christ Jesus, you are not going to walk in it. I would like you to know that God has a plan for you, and He is working it out, and it shall be manifested if you believe it and stay on course.

You may be worried that people may say something is wrong with you because you are this age and still unmarried. You may be worried about what everybody thinks. Please know that being unmarried does not mean there is something wrong with you; there is nothing to be ashamed of for being single. You may not think so, but believe me, some married people envy you; they envy your freedom and what God is doing in your life.

Another challenge for singles, where there is a child involved but the person is not married, is the tendency to start to see the child as a mistake and a stumbling block to getting married and finding happiness. If you believe in destiny, you will know that every human being is ordained by God. In destiny, it really does not matter how somebody was conceived; it could be through rape, an immoral relationship, or in whatever way; the truth remains that every child is conceived with the permission of God and is born to achieve something significant here on earth. No one person is the product of a mistake. If you are a single parent, know that your child is a gift and a blessing. Love your child, and be the best parent you can be; there is someone out there looking to live the rest of his life with you. You need to look to the future and forgive your past. God uses even our mistakes for His glory. It is a mistake for a believer to not want to marry somebody simple because he or she has a child.

Dealing with the Challenge of Loneliness

Loneliness is one of the common challenges I have seen among single believers, especially older ladies. I have talked with quite a few who said they cry in their beds at night; they just want to be with somebody. We all want somebody, we all want some sort of companionship, and most of us want to marry to satisfy that need. There is nothing wrong with wanting to be with somebody. Unless you feel like a eunuch or celibate, it is natural to want to have someone in your life; it can be tough when you do not have one. However, it is possible to enjoy life and have genuine satisfaction in life without having someone in your life. Your happiness should never depend on another person. You have got to devise a way of living life to the full by yourself, whether there is marriage or not. If you cannot deal with being single, you will become depressed and desperate. In desperation, you will lose your worth, you will lose your sense of judgment, and you will likely accept anybody for a marriage partner.

Many singles, especially older ones, have challenges when it comes to dealing with loneliness, with the feeling of unworthiness and rejection. The devil lies to them and says they are not good enough; that is why they remain single. You have got to kill that feeling of not being good enough. In dealing with loneliness, one fundamental thing is to find the love of God in your heart and develop the joy of fellowship with Him. Rediscover the joy of communal fellowship and the joy found in serving God, especially in church, and celebrate it. Meet people after church; don't just walk away home. Commit to your work or studies and get busy; this way, when you are back at home, you are tired and ready to go to bed. Don't live in a big house all by yourself; get people to live with and share your life with you. Make friends in church and at work and spend time with them. Socialise, meet people in the gym, attend work place parties and barbecues, and go on holiday with friends, especially those with Christian values. In your search for friendship and companionship, maintain your stand in the will of God, even when it feels difficult (but don't date on the Internet; this can lead to pain).

The Challenge of Family and Peer Pressure

Where I come from, when you reach a certain age and are still single, people wonder why; they think something is wrong with you, so they keep asking what is wrong. They can make you feel as though you are abnormal. Most times when you reach a certain age, family and friends put pressure on you to get married, and sometimes, they want to arrange a marriage for you. My advice is don't allow their pressure to get to you, or else you are likely going to marry somebody who is just going to cause you pain, somebody who really does not deserve you. Don't marry for anybody else's sake; don't let anybody make you do it, as nobody will help you live with the person. Don't marry just anybody so you can be with somebody; he may end up being a pain to you. Don't reduce your worth and allow feelings of shame to fester simply because somebody you know is married and you are still single.

Feel good about who you are, be proud of what God has helped you to achieve in your career or studies, be confident, be bold, and look to the future like you know that everything is going to work out for you the way God has planned it. Always remember, there is nothing abnormal about being single. Remember what the Apostle Paul says: *"I wish everyone could get along without marrying, just as I do. But we are not all the same. God gives some the gift of a husband or wife, and others he gives the gift of being able to stay happily unmarried. So I say to those who aren't married and to widows, better to stay unmarried if you can, just as I am"* (**1 Corinthians 7:7-8, TLB**).

Dealing with Sexual Desires as a Single Person

It is not a sin to have sexual desires; God created you to feel that way, so don't feel guilty if you have them. However, God wants us to satisfy those desires only within the context of marriage. **1 Corinthians 7:1-2** says, *"Now concerning the things whereof ye wrote unto me: It is good for a man not to touch a woman.*

Nevertheless, to avoid fornication, let every man have his own wife, and let every woman have her own husband." Therefore, we are to bring our body with all its desires under subjection to the will of God. See the following scriptures:

> *"But I keep under my body, and bring it into subjection: lest that by any means, when I have preached to others, I myself should be a castaway"* (**1 Corinthians 9:27**).

> *"Neither yield ye your members as instruments of unrighteousness unto sin: but yield yourselves unto God, as those that are alive from the dead, and your members as instruments of righteousness unto God"* (**Romans 6:13**).

Dealing with sexual desires can be a challenge to mature singles, especially if they have experienced the pleasure of sex before. It makes it even harder in this society, where we are being bombarded every day, everywhere, with sexual images. We see sexual images on television, on the Internet, on billboards, at the filling stations, just about everywhere. But God's grace is sufficient for you. The Bible says in **Romans 5:20**, *"Where sin abounded, grace abounded much more."* If you are having a challenge dealing with sexual issues, if you engage with sex toys, view pornography, masturbate, and so on, God can help you out. See your pastor, be open about it, and you will find help. Don't cover it up, trying to hide it, yet going about feeling guilty and not feeling confident to appear before God. Don't allow it to destroy your joy, your relationship with God, and your joy of serving God. Speak to your pastor about your challenges; he won't condemn you, he will want to pray with you. In all, keep in mind that it is a natural thing to have sexual desires, except if you are a eunuch or you have the gift of celibacy. So just having a sexual feeling does not mean you are ungodly, and there is no need for you to feel dirty or guilty as a result. However, you don't have to indulge in sex outside the boundaries God has put in place. Here are some guidelines to help you:

I. As a young person, see it as a spiritual duty to remain a virgin until marriage and trust God to preserve you and help you achieve. It can be a challenge to apply restraint once the boundaries have been crossed and you taste the forbidden apple. You may struggle with quenching the flame if you ignite its fire, so you must learn to say no and do all you can, trusting the Lord to keep you.

II. Have self-worth and dignity. Know that you are not cheap. Don't show yourself as loose, careless, or standardless. Don't project an attitude of "come have me if you want." Don't let anyone treat you like a piece of meat, like something to be used and dumped. Precious pearls cost a lot to find, and such are you. And don't be so in love with someone—no matter who he or she is—that you forget your standard and worth.

III. Make yourself accountable to someone other than a peer—someone older, of the same gender, a God-fearing mentor. He or she should be someone you can freely ask your questions to; share your feelings, fears, and thoughts with; and not feel dirty or judged by.

IV. Make it a principle not to feast your eyes on what can entrap and ensnare you. Watching sexy movies and looking at certain photos can wake the "monster" in you. You are to sieve what you watch on TV and where you go to on the internet. Your eyes are gateways, and through them your mind gets fed and your body is set in motion. The Bible says that if you want to keep your body in the light, you should keep your eyes single. *"The light of the body is the eye: therefore when thine eye is single, thy whole body also is full of light; but when thine eye is evil, thy body also is full of darkness"* (Luke 11:34). This advises you to keep your eyes focused only on the things you want to influence your behaviour. You are not going to be able to overcome sexual cravings and the like if you continue to feed your eyes with all the dirt on the internet and TV.

V. As a believer with godly values, avoid dating someone who has no relationship with Jesus—no matter who the person is and no matter what he or she brings. If all he or she wants from you is sex, walk away from the person. If he or she thinks the only way to show you value each other is by having sex, walk away. If he sees nothing wrong in having sex before you are married, walk away. Your relationship with God must be your highest priority.

VI. Know how to use your time efficiently. There is a saying: "idle hands are the devil's workshop." David fell into sexual sin with Bathsheba because he stayed back at home when he was meant to be at the battlefield (2 Samuel 11:1-5). Get busy every day investing your time, life, and resources into things that will impact your future. Don't idle away, wasting your precious time on things that wont add value to you. When you are busy, you get focused and single-minded. Don't procrastinate; take care of important things today and now. Don't go seeking fun where you can't afford it. To keep busy, try to cultivate the habit of reading books, and read a lot. If you are not in any employment, volunteer your time and service to a charity or other voluntary organization to keep busy and productive.

VII. The most important defence of all is disciplined lifestyle. You must have boundaries and keep to them. Know your red lines and no-go areas and adhere to them no matter the pressure. The Bible says no one puts fire in his bosom and doesn't get burnt (Proverbs 6:27). Don't toy with sin; it's not something you can tame. Make holiness your watch word. Don't cross your boundaries. Avoid sensual kissing and touches and fondling of the opposite sex; they can lead to what you don't want to do.

Don't expose yourself by staying with the opposite sex in dark corners or places where you make yourself vulnerable or by spending time together during "ungodly hours" with someone you have feelings for. A lot of the people who fell into sexual sin did not intentionally set out to commit such sin; they only violated their principles, stepped out of boundaries, and allowed room for the enemy to take advantage. That is why the Bible says to give the devil no foothold and to flee youthful lust (Ephesians 4:27; 2 Timothy 2:22).

The Challenge of Age Difference in Reverse

The general trend is that a man marries a woman who is younger than him (or at the least the same age). This is the normal trend in most cultures. As such, it is a challenge, especially, for ladies who have a younger man seeking their hand in marriage. Some men also have a problem with marrying a woman who is older than them. I am of the opinion that age should not be a barrier in marriage; God did not set that to be the standard. Some people think that it is abnormal or wrong for a lady to love and marry a younger man. I don't see anything wrong with that. I don't see anything wrong in a lady of forty marrying a man who is only thirty-three. I don't think there is anything wrong with it, but it can be a challenge.

Being realistic, the chances of a forty-five-year-old single lady finding a single man who is forty-seven or forty-eight years old and who has never married before are slim. Most men at that age are either already married or divorced. Ladies, there is nothing wrong in marrying a man younger than yourself. Men, there is nothing wrong in marrying somebody you love who is older than you. However, you ought to listen to what God is saying about your situation first. The Bible does not say it is wrong for a woman to marry a younger man.

> *"Amram married his father's sister Jochebed, who bore him Aaron and Moses. Amram lived one hundred and thirty-seven years"* (**Exodus 6:20**).

Amram gave birth to three great people: Miriam, Aaron, and Moses. Moses was one of the greatest men who ever walked this earth; he spoke with God face to face and performed some of the greatest miracles ever. Whatever the case, if you are going to marry a younger man, you should not just be trying to escape singleness. You should know that the man is responsible, somebody you are not going to treat like your little brother, but somebody you can respect, honour, and allow to be the head of the family, as God has said. No woman should marry anybody she will find it difficult to submit to.

Showing Yourself Available

Never forget this: God is faithful. He always brings people into our lives to establish what He has ordained. You will find that some people are single today, not because they had no one seeking a relationship with them, but because they made a shipwreck of what they had. They did not manage their relationship well, they pushed people away with their attitude, or they never wanted a relationship at the time it came.

In making yourself available, the first thing to know is that it is the man's duty to find a woman who is suitable for him. It is not for the woman to go looking for the man to marry. However, it is the woman's responsibility to put herself where she can be found. Remember Ruth and Boaz? From Ruth's account, we learn that by making yourself available, by learning to socialise, getting involved with people, and not living in isolation, you can play a significant part in him finding you. Let your life not be lived from work to home, television, and bed. Get involved with people at work, get involved with people in church, attend conferences, and don't limit them to ones put together by your church. You can't tell where he will find you.

I know there is somebody out there looking for you; maybe he has seen you in his dream and can't wait to meet you. Don't be somebody who sneaks into church late and leaves immediately after the grace; you need to socialise. Secondly, you must learn to never look down on anybody. Don't judge a man by what he has achieved, rather assess him by his passion and commitment to what he sees in the future.

Before you say no to a man, make sure that you have taken time to pray about it and have sought counsel from your pastor and are sure that he is not the man. Women often turn down their man of destiny and regret their decision when it is too late. If you met somebody you fancy or can see that he fancies you, don't make quick conclusions; the first thing to do is to show yourself friendly, approachable, and available. You don't know; he or she could be the right person. Don't give the "not cheap" or the "hard to get" impression. Even if your first impression is not positive, don't immediately push him away; try to show yourself friendly.

The hard-to-get attitude has sent away people with good intentions (even the right people, for that matter). Remember, **Proverbs 18:24** says, *"A man that hath friends must shew himself friendly: and there is a friend that sticketh closer than a brother."* Listen to me, ladies: most men do not speak about having a serious relationship because they are afraid of making a mistake in marriage; they are afraid of having a bad marriage. They are afraid of ending up with a difficult and complicated wife. A man will only propose when he is sure that she is kind, is respectful, and can be instructed. Your demeanour can confirm to the man that he has gotten it right, or it could drive him away. Somebody out there is looking for you, just you; help him to find you.

CHAPTER 5

Dealing with Conflict in Relationships

"If it be possible, as much as lieth in you, live peaceably with all men" (**Romans 12:18**).

We are all in some sort of relationship with somebody. It could be a spouse, a boyfriend or girlfriend, a colleague at work, a classmate, a roommate, or a neighbour. Relationships are beautiful experiences, and some are ordained by God. All relationships that are ordained by God are designed to empower us and help us become the people God created us to be. Once in a while, we experience conflict in our relationships. Conflicts don't just happen because we are in a relationship with the wrong person; they happen because of the human factor. We all make mistakes; we all get it wrong sometimes. Conflict means that there is a misunderstanding or a difficulty in your relationship or that you are having some sort of disagreement, and it is causing a rift between you and somebody you relate with. It is important that no matter what, we look for a way to deal with the conflict we have found ourselves in.

Working out peace in a challenging relationship is very important; don't ever say, "I don't care if he wants to leave; let him. I don't really care what happens." No! We are to pursue peace and pursue it hard, because destiny could be interrupted if there is a breaking away; what you could have achieved in a year might take you ten years to achieve as a result. The Bible says in **Romans 12:18**, *"If it be possible, as much as lieth in you, live peaceably with all men."* Making peace with all men implies that God desires that we make peace, even with our enemies, and He also says, *"When a man's ways please the Lord, he maketh even his enemies to be at peace with him"* (**Proverbs 16:7**). We are to do all we can to maintain peace and friendship with the people God has brought into our lives, especially with those in the brotherhood:

> *"With all lowliness and meekness, with longsuffering, forbearing one another in love; Endeavouring to keep the unity of the Spirit in the bond of peace"* (**Ephesians 4:2-3).**

We Have the Ministry of Reconciliation

We are called to make peace with people and to help them make peace with God and with others:

> *"And all things are of God, who hath reconciled us to himself by Jesus Christ, and hath given to us the ministry of reconciliation"* (**2 Corinthians 5:18**).

Making peace is a ministry; it is every believer's ministry. Making peace brings us to a place of peace, happiness, rest, and contentment. We don't need to fight battles, even with our enemies. God's best for us is that we dwell in the place of peace. Battles are destructive. They cause pain, heartaches, confusion, division, and a breaking away; these types of situations don't glorify God. When a believer finds himself in a conflict of any sort, he must seek a resolution and peaceful outcome. Being actively involved in pursuing peaceful outcomes whilst in any conflict makes us the children of God and witnesses to the world:

"Blessed are the peacemakers: for they shall be called the children of God" (**Matthew 5:9**).

It is really sad and unfortunate when believers find it difficult to resolve their issues amicably. It is sad to see a husband and wife who once enjoyed intimate moments together break up because they could not resolve their issues. It is also very unfortunate when two friends who have stood for each other for many years and have helped to contribute to what they have both become today look for ways to ruin each other and bring down what they have both worked so hard to build, only because they could not resolve their issues. Conflicts can be very painful and destructive when not resolved. The desire for a peaceful resolution when in conflict should come naturally to a believer; it does not matter who he is having the problem with. Jesus instructed us when He said:

"But I say unto you, love your enemies, bless them that curse you, do good to them that hate you, and pray for them which despitefully use you, and persecute you; That ye may be the children of your Father which is in heaven: for he maketh his sun to rise on the evil and on the good, and sendeth rain on the just and on the unjust" (**Matthew 5:44-45**).

How you relate with people shows whether you walk in the light or not. It does not matter if the people have shown themselves to be friends or enemies; it is your response that counts. By the believer having the ministry of reconciliation means that the onus is on the believer to seek reconciliation first when his relationship is tearing apart. Also it means that where there is strife and division between people, the believer is to look for ways to help to restore the relationship. We have the ministry of reconciliation. Believers should put value on all healthy relationships and should never be involved with stirring up strife amongst people or sowing a seed of discord. God sees that as an abomination and the person who does it as a perverse person. Watch how the Bible puts it:

> *"These six things doth the Lord hate: yea, seven are an abomination unto him: A proud look, a lying tongue, and hands that shed innocent blood, An heart that deviseth wicked imaginations, feet that be swift in running to mischief, A false witness that speaketh lies, and he that soweth discord among brethren"* (**Proverbs 6:14-19, KJV**).

This scripture mentions six things that God hates, and the seventh is what He calls an abomination. Now am going to list them out so you can see it.

A proud look
A lying tongue
Hands that shed innocent blood
A heart that devises wicked imaginations
Feet that are swift in running towards mischief
A false witness that speaks lies
He that sows discord among brethren

All the seven behaviours listed can damage any human relationship; God says He hates them, but He only calls the seventh one an abomination. An abomination is something that is vile, is detestable, is disgusting, and should be abhorred. Anything that is an abomination before God attracts curses. When you talk of abominable acts, what easily come to mind are things like incest, homosexuality, paedophilia, beastialism, and the like. But we can see that God has put sowing discord amongst brethren in the same category. Actually, the Bible says the person who stirs up conflict between people is perverse:

> *"A perverse person stirs up conflict, and a gossip separates close friends"* (**Proverbs 16:28, NIV**).

A perverse person is somebody who has no sense of decency, is immoral, is corrupted in his mind, and treats as normal what is shameful and forbidden. You must never put yourself in a place where you are responsible for the split of people who are in a healthy, godly, and fruitful relationship. Never be responsible for the break-up of anybody's marriage. Never be the cause of a fight between friends. Never be responsible for anybody's pain. When you know that what you are saying about that person will create a fight between him and somebody, why say it? When you know that what you are saying will create bitterness in somebody towards another, why say it? When you know that what you are saying will make somebody despise another person, why say it? Why talk about people behind their backs? If you don't like what you see, confront them but don't be a gossip, don't be a tale bearer, don't be perverse. You have no right to discuss a person with somebody else if you have not spoken to him first. You have no right to tell somebody what another person has said about him if you have not first challenged him.

Going behind a person and saying things about them, even if it is truthful, is gossip and can cause a rift in relationships. If somebody comes to tell you what somebody has said about you, you need to ask him what he did about it before coming to you. He is not trying to help you, his motive is wrong; he is only trying to portray that person as being bad. You do not need to hear everything that is said about you. This person who is telling you things about somebody is also going to go to tell another person what you said. Never say anything about anybody that you wouldn't like to be quoted as saying, especially if it concerns him; it's only going to create a rift. Be ready to stand by whatever you say; it should not matter who it concerns. Gossip is as terrible as stabbing a friend from behind; it can ruin a whole community.

Where people have no guard over their tongues, there is not going to be any genuine peace or trusting relationships; instead, you will find confusion, back-stabbing, and mistrust. The tongue is like a fire; it has set ablaze and ruined many homes, caused many hurts, and reduced the impact of many churches to such an extent that many have left feeling wounded and betrayed. I have seen that it is much easier to resolve conflict in any relationship where there are no gossips. When problems between people keep burning, and it becomes difficult to resolve, a lot of time it is because there are gossips who go behind people's backs to say things that are not helping. Watch how Bible puts it:

> *"Without wood a fire goes out; without a gossip a quarrel dies down"* (**Proverbs 26:20, NIV).**

If you want to enjoy a lasting union with anybody, you must decide not to listen to what anybody is saying about that person. And always remember that when somebody comes to you to say unhealthy things about a person you are in a relationship with, ask him what he has done about it before coming to you. If he has not first confronted the person, then he is not trying to help the situation or yourself; he only wants to paint him as being a bad person. And be careful with people who come to tell you things about people you care about and say, "But please don't let him know I told you."

Any Relationship Can Impact on Destiny

Relationships are beautiful, are inspiring, and are gifts from God. Having people in your life is one of the most wonderful blessings of living. Never forget that anybody who comes into your life can be a destiny helper, and you too could be the destiny helper to a person you have a relationship with. I once heard somebody say, "You have something that I don't have, I have something that you don't have, but together we can have everything. I can do something that you cannot do, you can do something that I cannot do, but together we can do all things." Conflict arises because of human limitations, and it can be a source of strength if dealt with correctly, but Satan likes to use it to cause confusion and pain and to separate people and keep their destiny from being fulfilled. Do what you can to maintain your relationships, and the beauty and pleasure that is in them will be released.

Conflict can make you ill; it can cause mental illness, depression, and heartache. It is difficult to live a peaceful and happy life when there is somebody in your life you cannot forgive or you are having a fight with. You can never fare well having bitterness inside you:

> *"For where envying and strife is, there is confusion and every evil work"* (**James 3:16**).

Conflict can hinder your prayer life, especially where you don't want to resolve it. That is why the Bible says, *"And whenever you stand praying, if you have anything against anyone, forgive him and let it drop [leave it, let it go], in order that your Father who is in heaven may also forgive you your [own] failings and shortcomings and let them drop. But if you do not forgive neither will your Father in heaven forgive your failings and shortcomings"* (**Mark 11:25-26**). If you can't forgive, God won't forgive you. If God won't forgive you, He won't bless you.

If unresolved, conflict can also stand in your way to heaven. You don't want to die with unresolved issues in your heart. The Bible says, *"Follow peace with all men, and holiness, without which no man shall see the Lord: Looking diligently lest any man fail of the grace of God; lest any root of bitterness springing up trouble you, and thereby many be defiled"* (**Hebrews 12:14-15**). According to the above scripture, bitterness can cause the grace of God to fail in a man's life. It also says that bitterness leads to trouble and defiles a man. This scripture is very clear about it; if you are not following peace with all men, you cannot see God. We therefore need to do our utmost to bring healing to our relationships that are going through a difficult period, for three reasons: firstly, so we can gain back our friend; secondly, for the sake of our relationship with God; and finally, so we can be sanctified and be healed.

Overcoming Evil with Good

God did not take us to heaven immediately after we got born again. We are still here and will continue to be until Jesus comes or we die. By the reason of our conversion and relationship with

Jesus, our lifestyle will be different from that of people who are not born again. The Bible says, though we are in this world, we are not of this world. If that be the case, then there is the likelihood that those who don't love God and don't appreciate our lifestyle are going dislike us, hate us, criticise us, or mock us. That was what Jesus was communicating to us when he said in **John 15:18-20**:

> "If the world hate you, ye know that it hated me before it hated you. If ye were of the world, the world would love his own: but because ye are not of the world, but I have chosen you out of the world, therefore the world hateth you. Remember the word that I said unto you, The servant is not greater than his lord. If they have persecuted me, they will also persecute you; if they have kept my saying, they will keep yours also."

We can only show that we are different from the rest of the word by how we react to those challenges and oppositions. If we were just to pay them back with the same coin, we would be no different from them. As we are still in this world, we are going to have to deal with the forces of darkness of this world. These forces inhabit humans and use those humans to try to disrupt our relationships. They will want to split friendships, split families, break up marriages, and wreck business ventures by driving the partners apart. We must know that we are never to engage in a fight with any human being when we are faced with these challenges but with the forces behind the people that the enemy Satan is using to achieve his intentions. The Bible says:

> "For we wrestle not against flesh and blood, but against principalities, against powers, against the rulers of the darkness of this world, against spiritual wickedness in high places" (**Ephesians 6:12**).

When confronted with conflict, you must always realise that it is Satan who is stirring it up. Satan likes to stir up conflict, because he understands the power that is in relationships. He knows that we all need each other to get to our destiny, and he wants to stop us from achieving our destiny by destroying our relationships. Satan also knows that the word of God says to follow peace with all men, without which no man shall see the Lord (**Hebrews 12:14).** Satan knows that as long as we are in contention with people and don't make it right, God will not answer our prayers, and we will not see God intervene in our situations. There is evil taking place all over the world. God wants us to live in victory over every evil design by the devil. There is no evil before a believer which he lacks the ability to handle, and it does not matter which way, shape, or form that it comes. We encounter evil at our work place, in our neighbourhood, in our schools, and so on. We are not to be conquered by evil, and we cannot overcome evil with evil but with good.

> "Do not be overcome by evil, but overcome evil with good" (**Romans 12:21, NKJV**).

You can't overcome darkness with darkness, fire with fire, anger with anger, or evil with evil. To deal with evil, you've got to choose to be good and walk in love with all men. We must be people who love people, irrespective of their background, colour, race, sex, or religious affiliation. We are not called to only love the brethren but all human beings, and we are not to treat any human being as an enemy, no matter what they do to us. People may see and treat you as their enemy, but you are not to see or treat anybody that way.

> "You have heard that it was said, 'Love your neighbor and hate your enemy.' But I tell you, love your enemies and pray for those who persecute you, that you may be children of your Father in heaven. He causes his sun to rise on the evil and the good, and sends rain on the righteous and the unrighteous. If you love those who love you, what reward will you get? Are not even the tax collectors doing that? And if you greet only your own people, what are you doing more than others? Do

not even pagans do that? Be perfect, therefore, as your heavenly Father is perfect" (**Matthew 5:43-48, NIV).**

Always Following the Way of Peace

You must give room for reconciliation and make way for peace whenever there is an interruption to your relationship with anybody. A believer must be seen to be the person who is offering peace when there is a conflict, and not the other way round. **Romans 12:18 (AMP)** says, "If possible, as far as it depends on you, live at peace with everyone." You show that you are seeking peace when you respond to people in an appropriate manner: in humility, with tolerance, and with respect. Never speak out of rashness, in anger, or in a revengeful way. Always make sure you are calm and in control, and choose your words carefully.

> *"My dear brothers and sisters, be quick to listen, slow to speak, and slow to get angry. Your anger can never make things right in God's sight. So get rid of all the filth and evil in your lives, and humbly accept the message God has planted in your hearts, for it is strong enough to save your souls"* (**James 1:19-27, NLT**).

How something is worded is vitally important. Many people don't know how to talk; they just say anything as it comes and do not bother about how it sounds in the ear of the other person. Some people think that by speaking exactly how they feel, they are being honest, not hypocritical and assertive, but actually, that only shows how immature they are and how they are not in control of their emotions or temperament. We must learn to be in control and should always carefully choose our words. Your ability to choose what to say, how to say it, when you say it, and who you say it to is a sign of maturity. I do not mean that you have to lie or not express yourself in a situation, but it is the manner in which you present what you have to say that counts.

"Those who consider themselves religious and yet do not keep a tight rein on their tongues deceive themselves, and their religion is worthless" (**James 1:26, NIV).**

"For in many things we offend all. If any man offend not in word, the same is a perfect man, and able also to bridle the whole body" (**James 3:2, KJV).**

The way we talk can either make way for peace or fuel the problem. There is a right time and a right way to say things. Learn it and practice it. When communicating, always make sure that whatever you say is clear, is filled with grace, is not spoken harshly or rudely, and as the Bible has said, is seasoned with salt. Always avoid getting mixed up in words. I mean never say what you would not like anyone repeating to a third party. Hold your peace if the conversation is turning to argument; don't let it get out of control. When you sense anger is rising in you, hold back; that is not the time to speak.

"My dear brothers and sisters, be quick to listen, slow to speak, and slow to get angry. Your anger can never make things right in God's sight" (**James 1:19-20, NLT**).

You can never say anything right when you handle it in anger. Try to keep prejudice, racism, or sentiment out; don't say, "Is it because I am black?", "Is it because I am a woman?", "It's like you are jealous," and so on. Also avoid using aggravating words like "Who do you think you are?" or "You shut up and listen." Never forget that the person you are speaking to is a human, precious in the sight of God, and has feelings too.

You Are the Light of the World and Salt of the Earth

"Ye are the light of the world. A city that is set on an hill cannot be hid. Neither do men light a candle, and put it under a bushel, but on a candlestick; and it giveth light unto all that are in the house. Let your light so

shine before men, that they may see your good works, and glorify your Father which is in heaven" (**Matthew 5:14-16, KJV).**

Never forget that in being light and salt, the people of the world must see a difference between you and them. Your behaviour and approach to situations must be a reflection of the life of God in you. For example, if a person is standing in your way to success, you must learn to support him where you can so he can succeed. When they curse you, you are to bless them. If a person is insulting and aggressive, to be different from him, you are to be calm and patient, turn the other cheek, and never pay back evil for evil.

> *"Recompense to no man evil for evil. Provide things honest in the sight of all men. If it be possible, as much as lieth in you, live peaceably with all men. Dearly beloved, avenge not yourselves, but rather give place unto wrath: for it is written, Vengeance is mine; I will repay, saith the Lord. Therefore if thine enemy hunger, feed him; if he thirst, give him drink: for in so doing thou shalt heap coals of fire on his head"* (**Romans 12:17-21**).

The right way to treat people who don't like you is to be good to them. When they are hungry, feed them; when they are thirsty, give them drink. Believers have the responsibility to use their capacity to walk in love with any person, irrespective of who they are or their actions.

Some Hints that Can Help when Dealing with Conflict

1) Understand that conflict is a human issue. It happens to all kinds of people; therefore, if you find yourself having to deal with conflict in your relationship, don't think it is unique to you. You should also realise that having conflict with somebody does not make you or the other person bad.

Human beings in a relationship can misunderstand each other; they sometimes disagree, make mistakes, stumble, and blow it. We all have the tendency to blow it. Though our actions could be wrong, a lot of times our heart might be right. The fact that you and that other person are having problems does not necessarily mean that you don't love each other, or that it is not the plan of God for you two to be together, or that you are a mismatch. No, it really does not mean that. When you understand these dynamics, you will make room for faults, you will not just condemn people for the slightest mistake, and you will be a bit more patient with them.

2) You need to rest in the truth that there is always a way out of every conflict. No matter what the problem is, don't see it as too huge and something beyond you to resolve; rather, reduce it to nothing. God will not allow anything that you can't handle to come to you. Know that God is bigger than any conflict you are ever going to face. Know that anything that He allows is a solvable matter, and you have the capacity to handle it.

In any case, you must rule out inviting the police or going to court, especially when it involves a brother. See **1 Corinthians 6:1-8.** First ask yourself, "Can this be resolved some other way without involving the police or the court?" To a believer, taking the matter to court should only be the last resort, after all options have been explored.

3) Take time to pray about the situation before you do anything about it. We are admonished in the scriptures to commit everything to God and seek His perspective before taking any action:

> "Trust in the Lord with all thine heart; and lean not unto thine own understanding. In all thy ways acknowledge him, and he shall direct thy paths. Be not wise in thine own eyes: fear the Lord, and depart from evil" (**Proverbs 3:5-7**).

If you have not talked to God and sought His grace about the conflict you are having in your relationship, you are likely not going to get God's perspective to it, and you are going to handle it in the wrong way. Taking your time to pray about it will also help you to calm down, develop peace in yourself, and not act out of rashness or anger. Anger never forges peace; you are never going to get it right and resolve anything with actions taken out of rashness:

> *"My dear brothers and sisters, be quick to listen, slow to speak, and slow to get angry. Your anger can never make things right in God's sight. So get rid of all the filth and evil in your lives, and humbly accept the message God has planted in your hearts, for it is strong enough to save your souls"* (**James 1:19-21, NLT**).

> *"A wrathful man stirreth up strife: but he that is slow to anger appeaseth strife"* (**Proverbs 15:18**).

Make sure you are always calm and in control and under God's influence before you start to deal with any conflict. If you have not dealt with the issue and resolved it within yourself, and you approach it while angry and with the thought of revenge, you will only complicate matters. Your anger can never make anything right in the sight of God. People often say and do things out of anger and then regret it later. But words are like vapour; once you let them out, you cannot withdraw them. What you say can have a hold on somebody, imprison them, and become damaging to them.

4) As a believer, you also need to understand the three stages of the Christian way to deal with conflict and commit to following these through. These stages are explained to us by our Lord Himself in **Matthew 18:15-17**:

> *"If your brother sins against you, go and show him his fault, just between the two of you. If he listens to you, you have won your brother over. But if he will not listen, take*

one or two others along, so that every matter may be established by the testimony of two or three witnesses. If he refuses to listen to them, tell it to the church; and if he refuses to listen even to the church, treat him as you would a pagan or a tax collector."

We will now look into each of these three stages and see how they work:

I. Your first step when dealing with conflict is to find an occasion to talk it through with your brother. The essence is to try to win him over and not to show him how bad or terrible you think he is. Don't keep hurts, bitterness, and grudges. Don't bottle it up until you can't take it anymore and then blow up. Don't start discussing the problem you are experiencing between you with others when you have not yet told him what he has done and how you feel about it. You will only make him look bad before others. The more a problem gets out and the more people are speaking into it, it becomes more complicated and difficult to solve. You are to do all you can to control it and keep it private, just between the two of you. The fewer people know of your problems, the more your chances of avoiding this escalation.

II. Your second step is to get two witnesses and take them with you to talk to the person; that should happen only if he won't listen to you in the initial stage. The witnesses are there to help resolve the issue by creating a neutral perspective to the whole matter and putting more pressure on the person. They are also there to serve as witnesses of how far you have gone to make peace. Never forget, though, that you are not to get people involved in your conflict until you have done the best you can to resolve it in private. What is also very important is your choice of witnesses. Your friend is likely to pay attention to them only if they appear neutral, not hostile, and if they are people he has respect for, people who can exert some influence on him.

III. Your third step is to bring the matter to the church, if he won't listen to you and your support team. The assumption is that a believer is somebody who should have high regard for the church and a deep-rooted respect for the authority of the church; a believer should see the church as representing Christ here on earth. It is Jesus' idea that a believer must belong to and be involved with a community of believers. It's not proper for a believer not to belong to any church. If you are reading this and don't belong to any church and don't have a pastor, you really need to go and do something about that. God wants you to have a pastor, someone you can feed on the Word from and receive spiritual guidance from:

> *"And I will give you pastors according to mine heart, which shall feed you with knowledge and understanding"* (**Jeremiah 3:15**).

I have seen problems easily get sorted out at this level. Many Christians will listen to their pastors and leaders. However, the Bible says to treat him as an unbeliever if he shows no respect to the authority of the church: for if he rejects the church, as it were, he rejects the authority of Christ. A man puts himself in a difficult position with God if he refuses to submit to following the Word of God. He takes himself out of God's commonwealth, he makes his prayers to be hindered and unanswered, and he exposes himself to all kinds of evil work.

> *"For where envying and strife is, there is confusion and every evil work. But the wisdom that is from above is first pure, then peaceable, gentle, and easy to be intreated, full of mercy and good fruits, without partiality, and without hypocrisy. And the fruit of righteousness is sown in peace of them that make peace"* (**James 3:16-18**).

Now, when your conflict is with somebody who is outside the church, and who has no regard for the authority of the church, your stage one and two will still apply. Your third stage may then be to completely ignore the person, treat it like it never happened, and move on with your life. In most cases, this is the best way to go about it, and hopefully the person would come to his senses some day and want to make it right with you. However, you may need to go to the law for adjudication. The Bible says it is wrong to go to the law only when your conflict is with a fellow brother. See **1 Corinthians 6:1-6**. You may have to go to court when you are dealing with somebody who is not a brother and you are left with no other options.

5) How you go about seeking reconciliation matters; it will determine whether you will achieve good results when you confront your brother or not. How you go about it can also complicate matters further. If your priority is to achieve peace, then you may need to start by first commending the other person for their contributions in your life. Nobody is totally bad; somehow and in some way, they have been good before. Commend him for it to start with; don't make it look like he is all bad and everything in your relationship is all bad. Remember, you are not out for a fight but resolution, and if you approach it that way, they will want to listen. Anybody will listen when they see that they are appreciated. Watch what the Bible says about the ideal approach:

> *"Let nothing be done through strife or vainglory; but in lowliness of mind let each esteem others better than themselves. Look not every man on his own things, but every man also on the things of others"* (**Philippians 2:3-4**).

6) You will also need to identify and take responsibility for your contribution to the problem and learn to say, "I am sorry." Always admit your contribution to the problem; don't appear holier than thou. Remember, it takes two to tango; admit it where you are wrong. Accept any blame for your part in the conflict and then give and seek forgiveness:

"Therefore, as God's chosen people, holy and dearly loved, clothe yourselves with compassion, kindness, humility, gentleness, and patience. Bear with each other and forgive whatever grievances you may have against one another. Forgive as the Lord forgave you" **(Colossians 3:12-13, NIV**).

7) It is important to understand that to resolve any conflict, you will need to show the other person that you hold them in high regard. Learning to talk in an appropriate manner to the person, no matter how hurt you feel inside, shows your regard for what you two have together. You are to maintain your respect and value for him as a person. The manner in which something is worded is vitally important when dealing with conflict. What we say and how we say it can fuel the problem or minister grace and peace.

Many people don't know how to talk; they just say anything as it comes out of reaction and do not bother about how it sounds to the other person or what it does to him. That is a hindrance to resolution. Words are powerful. They can either heal or cause damage. You always need to consider what impact your words will make on the person listening and whether you will achieve what you want to achieve as you speak. See what the following scriptures say:

"A soft answer turneth away wrath: but grievous words stir up anger" (**Proverbs 15:1**).

"There is one who speaks like the piercings of a sword, but the tongue of the Wise promotes health" (**Proverbs 12:18, NKJV**).

"Let your speech be always with grace, seasoned with salt, that ye may know how ye ought to answer every man" (**Colossians 4:5-6**).

When you show no regard with your use of words, you may drive people further away from you and increase the problem. When you eventually come to resolving any issues, you may end up digressing from what you really wanted to deal with, as other issues creep up from what was said and the way in which it was said. The wrong use of words can make matters worse.

8) Another very important thing when resolving conflict is the need to always avoid bringing up your conflict when there are people around. If you do, the other person may think that you are trying to shame him, disgrace him, or make him look bad before others. His reaction in that situation is likely to defend himself. You must make it a private matter in the initial stage. You also give people permission to get involved in your matter when you bring it up in the open. You must show restraint, patience, and respect. Here are two sayings that you could ponder on regarding this: "Don't open a can of worms" and "Don't wash your dirty linen in public."

9) To get it right with your friend, you must decide beforehand what you intend to achieve; you need to come to the table with an offer of mercy and not a fight. Your meeting must not be confrontational. While on the resolution table, your focus should be to resolve the current issue and to avoid unearthing matters that are in the past. Don't go reminding the person that he did the same thing ten years ago or the number of times he hurt you in the past. You are only going to digress, you will not effectively deal with what is at hand, and you will not achieve genuine reconciliation. You are to simply stick to the real issues at hand. Let the past always stay in the past, come with an offer of mercy and not a fight, and be open to understand the main cause of the problem; this will help you to find an effective and permanent resolution to your problems.

10) In relating with the person you are having problems with, you will need to work within the kingdom principle of

overcoming evil with good. The Bible says in **Romans 12:17-21** (**NKJV**), *"Repay no one evil for evil. Have regard for good things in the sight of all men. If it is possible, as much as depends on you, live peaceably with all men. Beloved, do not avenge yourselves, but rather give place to wrath; for it is written, 'Vengeance is Mine, I will repay,' says the Lord. Therefore if your enemy is hungry, feed him; if he is thirsty, give him a drink; for in so doing you will heap coals of fire on his head. Do not be overcome by evil, but overcome evil with good."* What this means is that whatever the situation is, you are to maintain a positive attitude and to keep being salt and light within that situation. The Bible admonishes us to not allow the sun to go down on your anger (**Ephesians 4:26**). What that means is that anger by itself is not sinful.

You are allowed to be angry but not to sin. You are committing sin when, as a result of anger, you are no longer shining your light, you are not behaving right, or you stop doing good things. That is what it means to not let the sun set on your anger. Being light means to walk in the footsteps of Jesus, not to stop loving, not to stop being kind or supportive, and to share even when you are angry and think the person does not deserve anything from you. If a person is not talking or sharing with you, you continue to talk and share with him. Instead of returning evil for evil and causing the problem to escalate, you can curtail it and overcome it by being good. Love can overcome anything. Anytime you are walking in love as opposed to evil, you attack that evil; evil can never overcome good. Also, evil can never be overcome with evil.

CHAPTER 6

Forgiveness and What It Can Do to You

"And hope maketh not ashamed; because the love of God is shed abroad in our hearts by the Holy Ghost which is given unto us" (**Romans 5:5**).

It is important to understand that there is a connection between our love walk and the operation of the Holy Spirit in our lives. The Bible says that God is *"able to do exceedingly abundantly above all that we ask or think, according to the power that works in us."* See **Ephesians 3:20**. That power is the Holy Spirit, because the Bible says, *"But you shall receive power when the Holy Spirit has come upon you"* (**Acts 1:8, NKJV**). Every believer has the Holy Spirit dwelling inside him (see **1 Corinthians 3:16).** The implication of this is that every believer has power. The indwelling of the Holy Spirit inside you is God's gift to you, to enable you to achieve His purpose for your life. That power inside you is there to enable you to fulfil your destiny. You can achieve the impossible; you can become all that God has said about you: for it is not by power nor by might but by the help of the Holy Spirit.

There is no limitation before the born again believer. The Holy Spirit that dwells within him can make anything possible.

However, the Holy Spirit is not moved by our worries, pains, or needs alone. He cares about them, but these things are not what stir Him up. He is only moved by our faith. So to get the Holy Spirit to move on your behalf, you will have to exercise your faith (see **1 John 5:4).** Your faith attracts and releases the Holy Spirit to work on your behalf. Moreover, you need faith to get the Holy Spirit to work for you, but it is important to also know that your faith is only alive and active when you are walking in love (see **Galatians 5:6**). What that means is that when you are not walking in love, your faith is dead and is not able to get the Holy Spirit to move.

The love of God is the Holy Spirit's atmosphere for miracles. He does not work where there is no love. It is possible for every child of God to experience miracles daily and to walk in the supernatural, but he will need to walk in love. Every believer has the capacity to love, because the Bible says, *"The love of God has been poured out in our hearts by the Holy Spirit"* (see **Romans 5:5, NKJV**). Actually, the evidence of being born again is the ability to love. Anybody who is not born again does not have the ability to love unconditionally (see **1 John 4:7-8).** If you are truly saved and have the Holy Spirit resident inside you, then you have the ability to walk in love. If you can walk in love, you have the ability to release the Holy Spirit and the power of God in every situation of your life.

Love Covers a Multitude of Wrongs

One fundamental thing about love is the power that it possesses to forgive. Forgiveness is one of the ways through which love expresses itself (see **Proverbs 10:12** and **1 Corinthians 13:4-7).** Forgiveness means to give mercy, kindness, compassion, or pardon where there is need for judgement. It also means to exonerate somebody from blame or guilt for the wrong he actually committed. Unforgiveness, on the other hand, means to deny somebody mercy, to hold him guilty for his wrong, and to subject him to the demand of justice. Unforgiveness is not the nature of God, and it is not the way of love. The power to forgive is inherent in love. If you have the love of God within you, then you have the power to forgive; there is nothing you cannot forgive. To a believer, forgiveness is a matter of choice. He can choose to forgive or choose not to forgive, just as he can choose to walk in faith or choose to walk in unbelief. But that is not the case with an unbeliever; he does not have the Holy Spirit inside of him and does not have the love of God in his heart and therefore cannot exercise the God kind of forgiveness.

Furthermore, no relationship can last a lifetime if the people in it cannot offer forgiveness. The fact is that nobody you are in a relationship with is perfect; there is a very high likelihood that they are going to do something stupid or wrong or offensive in one way, shape, or form, not because they set out to hurt you, but because people are not perfect. Imperfect people do wrong from time to time. Everybody has the tendency to hurt people, and we all need to learn how to deal with those hurts. The ability and willingness to offer forgiveness is vital, because without it, you are not going to be able to deal with hurts; rather, it is likely that you are going to destroy the relationship you have with somebody and walk away from people who matter to you.

When You Forgive, It Is for Your Own Sake

The Bible has said that God Himself forgives us our sins, for His own sake (**Isaiah 43:25**). He forgives us so that He can maintain a relationship with us. He has a father's heart and wants us to be His sons and daughters; if He cannot forgive us, He would have to cut us off and have nothing to do with us, but He does not want to do that. He forgives so that He can enjoy eternal fellowship with us. That is one of the reasons why He made us, so He can have a relationship with us. He forgives us so that He can bless us, as it is in His nature to bless. If God cannot forgive you, He will not bless you. That is why Jesus said when you pray, forgive if you have anything against anybody (see **Mark 11:24-25**). Forgiveness falls under the law of harvest; the law of harvest says to do unto others what you want done to you. The truth is that we all need forgiveness; we all sometimes do wrong.

Nobody stands uncondemned by himself before God. It follows, therefore, according to the law of harvest, that if there is anything that somebody did to you that you cannot forgive, then you should also expect God to hold something against you and cause you to walk in condemnation. The implication is that unforgiveness hinders your blessings. When you don't forgive people for whatever wrong or offence they have committed against you, God sees you as being wicked and will deal with you as with the wicked (see **Matthew 18:23-33**). Now you need to know how God deals with the wicked. The Bible says, "God is angry with the wicked every day." See **Psalm 7:11**. It also says God will not give peace to the wicked. See **Isaiah 48:22**. You really do not want God to be angry with you or to hold back His peace from you. When God withdraws peace from somebody, He releases him to the tormentors. Now let us look at the scripture that clearly explains this:

> "But the same servant went out, and found one of his fellowservants, which owed him an hundred pence: and he laid hands on him, and took him by the throat, saying, Pay me that thou owest. And his fellowservant fell down at his feet, and besought him, saying, Have patience with me, and I will pay thee all. And he would not: but went and cast him into prison, till he should pay the debt. So when his fellowservants saw what was done, they were very sorry, and came and told unto their lord all that was done. Then his lord, after that he had called him, said unto him, O thou wicked servant, I forgave thee all that debt, because thou desiredst me: Shouldest not thou also have had compassion on thy fellowservant, even as I had pity on thee? And his lord was wroth, and delivered him to the tormentors, till he should pay all that was due unto him. So likewise shall my heavenly Father do also unto you, if ye from your

hearts forgive not every one his brother their trespasses" (**Matthew 18:28-35, KJV**).

The tormentors are the demons behind sickness, the devourer, the spirits that are behind all kinds of misfortunes and losses. **James 3:16** says, *"For where envying and strife is, there are confusion and every evil work."* Where there is strife, you will find confusion and evil work. Bitterness, strife, and malice are all environments that breed evil. That is the devil's environment, where he is empowered and at liberty to operate. I have seen people who have ended up in the psychiatric ward because of bitterness. I have seen people lose their confidence, isolate themselves, even quit their jobs because they did not know how to deal with hurts.

I once prayed for a lady who said she became asthmatic a few days after her wedding. She shared a testimony with me of how she developed bitterness against her pastor because he would not support their wedding; as a result, they left him, married in another church, and withdrew their membership from that church. However, soon after wedding, she became asthmatic. She forgave the pastor that night as she went on her knees and asked God for mercy. While she prayed, the power of God fell on her like a burning sensation, and she was healed of the asthma instantly.

A few years ago, I was invited to pray for a lady who had just had a baby. She was supposed to be breastfeeding but had become mentally incapacitated and could not feed the baby or even pick him up. This lady was usually very pretty and well presented; however, she had started to look unkempt. She would not go outdoors and refused to speak to anyone, including her husband. I asked him how it all started, and he said she became angry with some people in her church. She asked her husband to leave that church, but he would not.

The husband also told us how God recently blessed them and increased them in wealth, such that they were able to refurbish their house, change their wardrobe, and buy a car. Soon after this, some people in church started to say that they had become worldly people; this offended his wife and made her bitter, which led to her condition. The bitterness gave the devil access to her. If the devil can find bitterness in somebody, he can attack their entire person, making them incapacitated and physically weak too.

There are many believers out there who do not see miracles in their lives simply because they will not forgive somebody. Unforgiveness will shut the windows of heaven against you. When you do not forgive, God will not fight your battles for you. When you are walking in unforgiveness with somebody, you are denying that person mercy and his blessing, especially that blessing which is meant to flow from you to him. You are not going to bless the person you hold grudges or malice against, are you? You are working against him if you can't bless him when you are supposed to; that is called vengeance. No one has the right of vengeance; it is God's prerogative. There are three cardinal things that God guards jealously and will never share with another man.

God's Three Cardinal and Exclusive Rights

The first is **His Godhood**. He says, *"I am the Lord thy God . . . thou shall have no other gods before me . . . for I the Lord thy God am a jealous God"* (**Exodus 20:2-5**). God is offended anytime somebody makes a god out of something in his life.

The second thing is **His glory**. He says, *"Thine O Lord is the glory"* (**1 Chronicles 29:11**) and also *"I will not give my glory unto another"* (**Isaiah 48:11**). When God is doing something, He wants to be recognised as the doer. He wants to take the glory for it all. He will not do anything that He will not take the glory for.

The third is **His right of vengeance**. He says, *"Vengeance is mine; I will repay, saith the Lord"* (**Romans 12:19**). God cannot tolerate you paying back evil for evil; that is exclusively His domain. You do not have the right to judge, and you do not have the right in Christ to pay back evil for evil. That is why He says:

> "Recompense to no man evil for evil. Provide things honest in the sight of all men. If it be possible, as much as lieth in you, live peaceably with all men. Dearly beloved, avenge not yourselves, but rather give place unto wrath: for it is written, vengeance is mine; I will repay, saith the Lord. Therefore if thine enemy hunger, feed him; if he thirst, give him drink: for in so doing thou shalt heap coals of fire on his head. Be not overcome of evil, but overcome evil with good" (**Romans 12:17-21**).

The Bible also says to *"bless them which persecute you; bless and curse not"* (**Romans 12:14**). If you want the Lord to withdraw from your fight, all you need to do is to step in the way and make the battle yours, and you will see Him withdraw. There are many ways you can step in the Lord's way: by withholding somebody's blessing, by standing in the way of somebody's progress, by doing something that will lead to somebody's downfall, by refusing to pray for somebody so he can be saved, by pronouncing a curse on somebody, by celebrating somebody's downfall. God said we must never rejoice when our enemy falls. See **Proverbs 24:17-18**.

God's Kind of Forgiveness

In relation to forgiveness, the Bible urges that we should be forgiving of one another, as God has forgiven us for Christ's sake (see **Ephesians 4:31-32**). Forgiveness is not really complete until it is done in the way that God in Christ forgave us. The human would say, "I have forgiven him, but I cannot forget what he did." Sometimes you hear people say, "Because he did this and that before, and though I know in my heart that I have actually forgiven him, and I am not going to do anything about it again, however, I am going to try to be wiser next time, watch him closely, and not allow him to take advantage of me again." What they are saying is, "I am going to try to avoid him or deal with him at arm's length so I don't get hurt again." That is how the carnal man understands forgiveness, but that is not the God kind of forgiveness.

How did God forgive us? He forgave all and took it out of the way (see **Colossians 2:13**). He not only forgave all, He also blotted out every record and ordinance which was contrary to us (see **Colossians 2:14**). He declared us free from the consequences of our sins. In other words, He says that we are no longer guilty of the sins we committed and are therefore not answerable for them (see **Colossians 1:21-22**). He renewed His thoughts towards us by taking out of His mind the record of our sin (**Isaiah 43:24**, **Jeremiah 31:34**, **Hebrews 10:17**). He filled His thoughts with only good things concerning us (**Jeremiah 29:11**, **3 John 2**).

If we will obey God and forgive those who have wronged us as He forgave us for Christ's sake, we will not lack anything good, we will not walk in affliction, and He will bless everything that we put our hands on. Forgiving somebody God's way means you are going to wipe out every record of wrong you hold against him, you are going to declare him free from the consequences of an action, you are also going to remove the thing that has kept you apart and start to treat him like he has never done it. That is the kind of forgiveness God showed us, and He desires us to do the same.

CHAPTER 7

Walking in Favour with God and Man

"Now when the turn of Esther, the daughter of Abihail the uncle of Mordecai, who had taken her for his daughter, was come to go in unto the king, she required nothing but what Hegai the king's chamberlain, the keeper of the women, appointed. And Esther obtained favour in the sight of all them that looked upon her. So Esther was taken unto king Ahasuerus into his house royal in the tenth month, which is the month Tebeth, in the seventh year of his reign. And the king loved Esther above all the women, and she obtained grace and favour in his sight more than all the virgins; so that he set the royal crown upon her head, and made her queen instead of Vashti" (**Esther 2:15-17**).

Looking at the above passage and the beautiful story of Queen Esther, you would see that King Ahasuerus did not choose Esther to be his queen because she was the most beautiful of all the women in the kingdom; neither did it say that she was chosen because the king saw she came from one of the most important families in his kingdom. Esther became queen in Vashti's place because she obtained more grace and favour than all the other virgins. It is worth highlighting that all the women presented before the king were virgins, but God's favour was the dividing line. Esther had it, and it lifted her above them all.

In the light of the favour of God, it is not what you have that counts, but His goodness towards you. One favour from God can transform your life and change your testimony. Favour comes in different dimensions; it can be a good deed or an act of kindness to somebody who does not deserve it. It is also about treating somebody preferentially. To walk in favour with God and man, therefore, means that both God and men will do good deeds to you or show you kindness beyond what you deserve. It means that in the midst of others, you will be preferred when there is no other reason than favour.

When you operate under favour, God's favour especially, your achievement, your promotion, and your increase will not be based on your qualifications or on your effort or on what you can or cannot do. When it is about favour, your qualifications will be immaterial, your effort will be immaterial, your gender will be insignificant, your background will be irrelevant, and the things you have been through will not count. That is not to say that we should not work hard to have the right qualifications. It is good to have qualifications, but where God's favour is concerned, your qualifications will not matter, and these will not determine the height you are going to rise to in life. You can be a college drop-out and still end up being the chief executive of a multi-million-pound software company.

Favour can lift someone who appeared to have nothing to a place of significance and influence. Without favour, even with the right qualifications, you can still get stuck in life and make no meaningful progress. Without favour, even with your hard work, you can have enemies who will make your life a misery. Without favour, even with a privileged background, you can become a waste of space, become depressed, and make a shipwreck of everything. It is good to be hard working, it is good to be connected to the right people in life, and it is good to have all the qualifications, but it is even better to walk in God's favour.

Favour will make all the difference you need. There are things that hard work cannot give you but favour will. There are places that qualifications cannot take you but favour will. Through God's favour, you can enter a realm you do not qualify for. For instance, Israel inherited cities they did not build. See how one of the great kings of Israel put it:

> "We have heard with our ears, O God, our fathers have told us, what work thou didst in their days, in the times of old. How thou didst drive out the heathen with thy hand, and plantedst them; how thou didst afflict the people, and cast them out. For they got not the land in possession by their own sword, neither did their own arm save them: but thy right hand, and thine arm, and the light of thy countenance, because thou hadst a favour unto them" (**Psalm 44:1-3**).

God is the Lord of the ends of the earth. He can lift up one and bring down another. He can kill and can make alive. When He blesses, no one can curse. He can make ways where there are no ways. He can make a poor man a wealthy man. He can make a failure very successful and accomplished. He can make the barren a mother of nations. There is nothing impossible with Him, and there is nothing you can ever desire that is beyond Him. If God favours you, there will be nothing to stop you. I pray that as you read along, you will connect with the God of favour, and I pray that He will make His face to shine on you. In Jesus' name. Amen.

When you have favour and are walking in it, you will notice that doors will start to open for you where they are shut against others. In other words, where they said no to other people before, they will say yes to you. What was not possible for someone else will become your reality. You will make little effort and reap in abundance even where others have laboured before and reaped nothing. Things will just work out for you, where others are finding it difficult. Not because you are necessarily doing anything different, but because Almighty God is shining upon you. God's favour can also make you enjoy His provisions; needs in your life will be met supernaturally. Strangers will bless you. By strangers, I mean people you do not know or have any relationship with; people you do not deserve assistance from will be there for you. With favour, you also won't have to worry about what any man will do to you, for He will make even your enemies to be at peace with you (see **Proverbs 16:7**).

After over four hundred years of Israel's sojourn in the land of Egypt and slavery to the Pharaoh, on the night that God was going to give them deliverance and bring them out of Egypt, God said to Moses to tell all Israel to ask of their neighbours for silver, gold, and precious raiment, for God wanted Egypt to pay back the children of Israel in one night for all the years of forced labour. God said to Moses concerning Israel:

> *"And I will give this people favour in the sight of the Egyptians: and it shall come to pass, that, when ye go, ye shall not go empty"* (**Exodus 3:21**).

Naturally, Egypt would not be blessing Israel the night they left, for they had just lost all the firstborn of man and beast in the land. As such for the sake of Israel, their God (the Lord Almighty) killed them to compel them to release His people. Naturally, Egypt should be stoning Israel in retaliation, but they blessed them instead. Why was this so? Because God gave them favour, for the scripture says:

> *"And the children of Israel did according to the word of Moses; and they borrowed of the Egyptians jewels of silver, and jewels of gold, and raiment: And the Lord gave the people favour in the sight of the Egyptians, so that they lent unto them such things as they required. And they spoiled the Egyptians"* (**Exodus 12:35-36**).

God's favour will make even your worst enemy to be on your side, and where enemies set traps for you, their traps will only be a stepping-stone to the next level, if God's favour is on your life.

Come with me to look at two people in the Bible who enjoyed God's rich favour working in their lives. These two people are Samuel, the prophet, and the Lord Jesus. Let us see what they did that attracted God's favour to them.

The Experience of Samuel the Prophet

From the scripture, we can see that Samuel attracted God's favour to his life because he grew before the Lord and served Him faithfully:

> *"And the Lord visited Hannah, so that she conceived, and bare three sons and two daughters. And the child Samuel grew before the Lord"* (**1 Samuel 2:21**).

> *"And the child Samuel grew on, and was in favour both with the Lord, and also with men"* (**1 Samuel 2:26**).

Samuel Grew before the Lord

Growing before the Lord means that Samuel developed a relationship with God. He spent time not only knowing about God, but knowing God and having an intimate relationship with Him. God desires that we create quality time to be with Him. There are very few people in church who really know God. There is a lot about His being and His essence that He wants to show us. He wants us to be able to know His voice, His ways, and His acts.

There is a favour that comes with a relationship: you treat some people in your life differently and with special consideration just because of who they are to you. In the same vain also, a deeper relationship with God attracts His favour. The more intimate you get with God, the more of Him and His help you will experience. To develop an intimate relationship with Him, you need to love Him more than you love anything of this life, create quality time to be with Him, and be willing to lay down anything for Him.

Samuel Ministered before the Lord

> *"And the child Samuel ministered unto the Lord before Eli. And the word of the Lord was precious in those days; there was no open vision"* (**1 Samuel 3:1**).

Samuel ministered unto the Lord. The word "minister" simply means "to serve." To serve God involves our willingness to offer unto Him our time, our worship, our possessions, and even our lives. Every believer I have known says, "I love God more than anything." However, it is one thing to say it and another to show it. I have seen very few people who will do anything for God, irrespective of the cost. If we do not hold anything from God, He will bless us with everything. True service is seen in our willingness and ability to lay down anything for somebody. Gifts have a way of opening up people's favour towards you. If you know how to give, you will attract favour. When you give to God, you attract God's favour, and when you give to man, you attract man's favour. That is why the Bible says:

> *"A man's gift maketh room for him, and bringeth him before great men"* (**Proverbs 18:16**).

Giving is a way of serving, and if you are a giver, it will surely make room for you and bring you before great men. Jesus taught this principle of gifts making room before great men in the parable of the rich man and his steward (**Luke 16:1-9**). Your gifts will definitely make room for you; if you are giving to God, it will make room for you before God. When Abraham ministered to God (the sacrifice of Isaac), God made a promise under an oath to him, saying, *"Blessing I will bless you, and multiplying I will multiply your descendants"* (**Genesis 22:1-18**). On the night that Solomon dedicated the temple to God, he made sacrifices of burnt offerings to God; the Lord, as a consequence, appeared to him in the night and asked what he wanted God to do for him (**2 Chronicles 7:1-5**). There is a blessing that comes with our willingness to give our all to the Lord.

In the Footsteps of Jesus

It is written that Jesus *"increased in wisdom and stature, and in favour with God and men."* See **Luke 2:52**. We will delve further into this scripture and learn from the life and character of our Lord.

The Wisdom of Jesus

Jesus attracted favour from both God and man because He grew in stature and increased in wisdom. Wisdom means to have the fear of God. **Job 28:28** says, *"And unto man he said, Behold, the fear of the Lord, that is wisdom; and to depart from evil is understanding."* The fear of God does not mean to be scared of God; instead, it means to have respect and reverence for Him. We need to hold God in awe. He is the Almighty God, the creator, the one who can make alive and can kill, and the one who is a consuming fire.

We express our fear of God through our love for righteousness and hate for evil, for it says in **Proverbs 8:13**, *"The fear of the Lord is to hate evil: pride, and arrogance, and the evil way, and the froward mouth, do I hate."* Now if wisdom means to have the fear of God and the fear of God means to hate evil, then we can deduce that the increase of wisdom that Jesus had means that as He was growing in His human form, He developed hatred for evil and a deep love for righteousness. And as a result of His love for righteousness and hatred for evil, God anointed and favoured Him. For the Bible says:

> *"But unto the son he saith, Thy throne O God is for ever and ever: a scepter of righteousness is the scepter of thy kingdom. Thou hast loved righteousness, and hated iniquity; therefore God, even thy God, hath anointed thee with the oil of gladness above thy fellows"* (**Hebrews 1:8-9**).

When you walk in the fear of God, He will show you His favour, anoint you in a special way, and enable you to achieve what you cannot achieve by your own strength. Never forget, the love for righteousness and hatred for evil will endear a man to God, and His favour will be towards him.

Jesus Grew in Stature

Growth in stature deals with your physical build, height, or physique. Jesus did not only increase in wisdom, He also increased in stature. God desires that we all move from being spiritual babies to spiritual adults, from carnal Christians to spiritual Christians. **1 Peter 2:2-3** says, *"As newborn babes, desire the sincere milk of the word, that ye may grow thereby: If so be ye have tasted that the Lord is gracious."* God, like every father, is pleased when we are growing spiritually, are developing muscles, and are being deep rooted in the kingdom. He needs us to grow, because there are certain benefits of the kingdom that we cannot enter into as babies. The anointing to receive them can only come on us when we grow to certain spiritual levels:

> *"Now I say, That the heir, as long as he is a child, differeth nothing from a servant, though he be lord of all; But is under tutors and governors until the time appointed of the father"* (**Galatians 4:1-2**).

At what point can we say that one has spiritually grown up? It is at the point where he has overcome things like envy, strife, and division, when he can no longer keep bitterness, hurts, and unforgiveness in his heart:

> *"And I, brethren, could not speak unto you as unto spiritual, but as unto carnal, even as unto babes in Christ. I have fed you with milk, and not with meat: for hitherto ye were not able to bear it, neither yet now are ye able. For ye are yet carnal: for whereas there is among you envying, and strife, and divisions, are ye not carnal, and walk as men"* (**1 Corinthians 3:1-3**).

A believer can also be said to have grown up when he starts to feed on strong meat. By strong meat, it means that the believer's spiritual senses are now developed, and he now has a good understanding of the things of God. He no longer solely depends on what others teach; he is now able to feed from the Word of God for himself and discern the ways of the Spirit by himself. Nothing from the Word can choke him, meaning he can now take in the rebukes, the corrections, and the call for a life of holiness and sacrifices and not just the "bless me", "give me," and "deliver me" material. At this stage, his behaviour is shaped solely by the Word and not by what somebody has said.

Having a Deeper Relationship with God

The kind of relationship we have with God and our attitude towards Him can affect how much of God we will have in our life, and it can affect the power and the effectiveness of our prayers. Many believers' prayers are not answered because of their attitude towards God. Our attitude towards God and towards the things of His kingdom determines our spiritual environment. Our spiritual environment determines the level at which God can work with us or for us. The first thing you must understand is that an unsaved person has no claim on God until he repents. Yes, I understand that the grace of God has appeared to all: hence, I know that there are certain things that the good God does to both the unsaved and the saved alike, like making sure your daily basic needs are met, helping you arrive safely after a journey, and so on. He does these things in His capacity as the creator (**Matthew 5:45**).

However, you must know that there are certain interventions of God that can happen to a man only as a result of his covenant relationship with Him, like God answering prayer, like God taking over and fighting his battles, like God supernaturally intervening for him in difficult times. Moreover, you must not base your relationship with God on what you can get from Him. Your primary focus on your relationship with God should not be about breakthroughs and miracles. Don't make serving God or being a Christian about what you can get out of Him; there is much more to it than that. There is something about knowing God that is much more than anything you can ever have or become in this world.

God wants to bless you materially, but He does not want you to be materialistic. Paul says in **1 Corinthians 15:19**, *"If in this life only we have hope in Christ, we are of all men most miserable."* You need to have a clear understanding of God, His glory, and His majesty. You need to understand the value of being in a relationship with the majestic God and what a privilege that is. If you know the value of your relationship with God, God will be the priority, and you are not going to do your own thing and only remember God and come to Him when you have worries and needs. You must make God the first passion in your life and strive to have an everyday relationship with Him.

The problem with the majority of Christians today is that they are too lazy or too busy to create time to be with God. They want the crown but not the cross. They are "fast-food" Christians, "microwave" Christians, always in a hurry when it comes to the things of God. They want to breeze in and out of God's presence with their entire shopping list, filled out to the brim. God did not save you so that He can be your consultant, so don't treat God like a consultant. He saved you so that you can have and enjoy fellowship with Him. He wants to spend time with you. Creating time to study the Word is also very vital in a believer's relationship with the Lord.

The knowledge of the Word enlightens us more about God, it unveils God's plan for our lives, and it also empowers our prayer life. That was why Jesus said, *"If ye abide in me, and my words abide in you, ye shall ask what ye will, and it shall be done unto you"* (**John 15:7**). When you abide in Jesus, that gives you a legal standing before God the Father. When you have God's Word in you, your prayers will be in accordance with what He says and in line with His will for your life.

You also need to strive to be a fruitful Christian. Being a fruitful Christian is about getting involved in God's kingdom business, like sharing the gospel with others, visiting the sick and the widow, visiting those in prison, and caring for the homeless and the orphans. It is about giving to the poor. It is about supporting those in full-time ministry in any way possible, and it is about funding the spread of the gospel. I believe that God is honoured when we serve Him in this capacity. I believe that the only reason God did not take us to heaven the day we gave our lives to Jesus is because He wants us to contribute something to humanity, and He wants us to be a blessing to our communities and our generation.

Loyalty Attracts Favour

Loyalty is a virtue that surely attracts favour anywhere. There are very few people who understand loyalty. You cannot count on many people these days when it comes to being loyal. When we are loyal to someone, we attract their favour. Loyalty involves sticking with people when it is going well with them and when it turns sour. You cannot be loyal when you keep changing your allegiance. Loyalty is about sticking up for people and defending them, even when you know they are in a mess that they caused themselves. The people you believe in will always make mistakes, but don't join others to stab them. That is being disloyal. Loyalty is about being available for people when they need you the most.

Loyalty is about making sacrifices for people even when it is costly to do so. It is always costly to be loyal, but when you are loyal to people, they will want to do anything for you too. If I may ask, how would you treat a person who is always there when you need help? How would you treat the people who when you need someone to go the extra mile, they are the ones doing it?

How would you treat people you know have your best interests at heart and will always be there for you? How would you treat people you know are not going to jump out of the boat and leave you to fight it alone when it is rough? How would you treat people who will always create time for you when you need them, who every now and then make contributions to increase your worth? How would you treat such people in comparison to others? Surely it will be preferentially. As a pastor, I know that there are people who can call me anytime, and it does not matter when I went to bed that night, I would jump up for them. Why is that so? Because one good turn deserves another. Loyalty attracts favour.

Mercy and Truth Attracts Favour

> *"Let not mercy and truth forsake thee: bind them about thy neck; write them upon the table of thine heart: So shalt thou find favour and good understanding in the sight of God and man"* (**Proverbs 3:3-4**).

When you are merciful towards people, you will always find favour in return. Don't be hard on people; always show mercy and kindness, and give a little help when you can. God in turn will surround you with favour. Be good to people, and I mean everybody you come in contact with, and who knows? You might be doing good to the angel of your destiny. The person you are being good to today may be in a privileged place tomorrow and in a position to do you a little favour in return. There is a profound quote that says, "Treat with kindness the people you meet on your way to the top, as you may meet them again on your way down." A scripture in Proverbs puts it this way:

> *"A good man obtaineth favour of the Lord: but a man of wicked devices will he condemn"* (**Proverbs 12:2**).

Also, don't live a false life; be honest with people, and deal with them with truth and integrity. If people can trust you, they will stick with you, they can recommend you, they can speak for you. If they are in a privileged position, they can be of great assistance to you, simply because the other day you dealt with them with integrity. Don't think because you are cunning and deceptive and are getting away with it, then it means that you are clever. No, the Bible says you are only being foolish. It will eventually work against you. **Proverbs 19:1** says, *"Better is the poor that walketh in his integrity, than he that is perverse in his lips, and is a fool."* If you want to attract favour to your life, you have got to be truthful with people.

I close with a story a friend told me about a boiled seed:

Once there was an emperor in the Far East who was growing old and knew it was coming time to choose his successor. Instead of choosing one of his assistants or one of his own children, he decided to do something different. He called all the young people in the kingdom together one day. He said, "It has come time for me to step down and to choose the next emperor. I have decided to choose one of you." The kids were shocked. But the emperor continued, "I am going to give each one of you a seed today. One seed. It is a very special seed. I want you to go home, plant the seed, water it, and come back here one year from today with what you have grown from this one seed. I will then judge the plants that you bring to me, and the one I choose will be the next emperor of the kingdom."

There was one boy named Ling who was there that day, and he, like the others, received a seed. He went home and excitedly told his mother the whole story. She helped him get a pot and some planting soil, and he planted the seed and watered it carefully. Every day he would water it and watch to see if it had grown. After about three weeks, some of the other youths began to talk about their seeds and the plants that were beginning to grow. Ling kept going home and checking his seed, but nothing ever grew. Three weeks, four weeks, five weeks went by. Still nothing. By now others were talking about their plants, but Ling didn't have a plant, and he felt like a failure. Six months went by, still nothing in Ling's pot. He just knew he had killed his seed. Everyone else had trees and tall plants, but he had nothing. Ling didn't say anything to his friends. However, he just kept waiting for his seed to grow.

A year finally went by, and all the youths of the kingdom brought their plants to the emperor for inspection. Ling told his mother that he wasn't going to take an empty pot. But she encouraged him to go, and to take his pot, and to be honest about what happened. Ling felt sick to his stomach, but he knew his mother was right. He took his empty pot to the palace. When Ling arrived, he was amazed at the variety of plants grown by all the other youths. They were beautiful, in all shapes and sizes. Ling put his empty pot on the floor, and many of the other kids laughed at him. A few felt sorry for him and just said, "Hey, nice try."

When the emperor arrived, he surveyed the room and greeted the young people. Ling just tried to hide in the back. "My, what great plants, trees, and flowers you have grown," said the emperor. "Today, one of you will be appointed the next emperor!" All of a sudden, the emperor spotted Ling at the back of the room with his empty pot. He ordered his guards to bring him to the front. Ling was terrified. *The emperor knows I'm a failure!* he thought. *Maybe he will have me killed!* When Ling got to the front, the emperor asked his name. "My name is Ling," he replied. All the kids were laughing and making fun of him. The emperor asked everyone to quiet down. He looked at Ling and then announced to the crowd, "Behold your new emperor! His name is Ling!"

Ling couldn't believe it. He couldn't even grow his seed. How could he be the new emperor? Then the emperor said, "One year ago today, I gave everyone here a seed. I told you to take the seed, plant it, water it, and bring it back to me today. But I gave you all boiled seeds, which would not grow. All of you, except Ling, have brought me trees and plants and flowers. When you found that the seed would not grow, you substituted another seed for the one I gave you. Ling was the only one with the courage and honesty to bring me a pot with my seed in it. Therefore, he is the one who will be the new emperor."

Giving men and women the resources and tools to succeed in life and fulfil the reason for which they were created.

www.victory-assembly.org
pastormusa.com

Destiny Is Within You—Overcoming All Obstacles and Embracing Success is a proven-successful guide that enables you to achieve the goals you set for yourself in life. You will discover that God created you for a specific purpose—and you exist to accomplish your God-given destiny.

You are not a loser, a burden, or a pest. You are a unique person with special talents and gifts, and you can enjoy a wonderfully abundant life—no matter your background, education, or current economic situation.

Destiny Is Within You reveals how:

- God created you to fulfill an exciting and prosperous purpose.
- To recognize and release your potential.
- Every idea, ambition, and dream in your heart is achievable.

The choices you make every day determine what you will become. You can choose to be a success or a failure, a winner or a loser, a person of honor or dishonor. This book explains clearly how you can make healthy choices and fulfill your destiny.

Musa Bako is the senior pastor of Victory Assembly, The Redeemed Christian Church of God, in Sheffield, United Kingdom. Together with his wife, Pastor Eunice Bako, they lead a dynamic, growing multicultural ministry. He is also a zonal coordinator within the RCCG network and a sought-after conference speaker. With more than 20 years in ministry, Pastor Bako has taught the Word of God worldwide. The Bakos are blessed with three children: Dorcas, Melissa, and Jethro.

"Changing the World, One Book at a Time."
www.evangelistamedia.com

DESTINY Is Within You

BAKO

overcoming all obstacles
and embracing success

DESTINY
Is Within You

Musa Bako

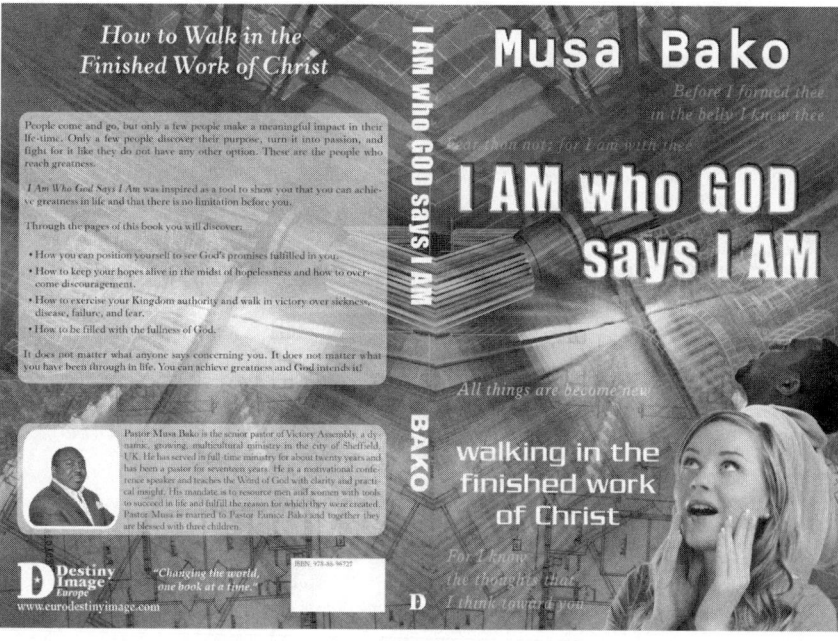

How to Walk in the Finished Work of Christ

People come and go, but only a few people make a meaningful impact in their life-time. Only a few people discover their purpose, turn it into passion, and fight for it like they do not have any other option. These are the people who reach greatness.

I Am Who God Says I Am was inspired as a tool to show you that you can achieve greatness in life and that there is no limitation before you.

Through the pages of this book you will discover:

- How you can position yourself to see God's promises fulfilled in you
- How to keep your hopes alive in the midst of hopelessness and how to overcome discouragement.
- How to exercise your Kingdom authority and walk in victory over sickness, disease, failure, and fear.
- How to be filled with the fullness of God.

It does not matter what anyone says concerning you. It does not matter what you have been through in life. You can achieve greatness and God intends it!

Pastor Musa Bako is the senior pastor of Victory Assembly, a dynamic, growing, multicultural ministry in the city of Sheffield, UK. He has served in full-time ministry for about twenty years and has been a pastor for seventeen years. He is a motivational conference speaker and teaches the Word of God with clarity and practical insight. His mandate is to resource men and women with tools to succeed in life and fulfill the reason for which they were created. Pastor Musa is married to Pastor Eunice Bako and together they are blessed with three children.

Destiny Image Europe
www.eurodestinyimage.com

"Changing the world, one book at a time."

ISBN 978-88-96727

D

Musa Bako

Before I formed thee in the belly I knew thee

I AM who GOD says I AM

All things are become new

walking in the finished work of Christ

For I know the thoughts that I think toward you

I AM who GOD says I AM

BAKO

Spine

The Love of Father God

Musa Bako

Front cover

FOREWORD BY ENOCH A. ADEBOYE

THE *Love*
OF *Father*
God

understanding the priesthood of Jesus,
the mystery and power of faith,
and the victorious life you can live now

Musa Bako

ABOUT THE AUTHOR

Pastor Musa Bako is the senior pastor of Victory Assembly RCCG in the city of Sheffield, UK. Together with his wife, Pastor Eunice Bako, they lead a dynamic, growing multicultural ministry, through which God is greatly impacting the people of Sheffield with the good news of Jesus. He is also a zonal coordinator within the RCCG network and sought after as a conference speaker.

With the grace of God on his life, and over twenty-three years in full-time ministry, Pastor Musa teaches the word of God with maturity, clarity, and practical insight to help people experience the life-transforming power of God for victorious living. His messages and writings cut across cultural boundaries, and he has been an encouragement and a blessing to people from all the continents of the world. Pastor Musa and Eunice are blessed with three children: Dorcas, Melissa, and Jethro.

ABOUT THE BOOK

Everybody Needs Somebody is written to empower you with tools to achieving a healthy and fruitful relationship in all spheres. There is something good in everybody. Everybody has something to offer the world. Everybody can be a blessing to someone. Everything God has ever made has value, is beautiful, and has a purpose.

In this book, you will discover:

- there is a purpose for your existence, you can know your purpose and can achieve it
- you need people to become what God intended for you to be
- God does not bring people together just for the sake of it; everybody you come in contact with has something to do with your destiny
- multi-cultural and multi-racial relationships are God's idea; we may look different from each other but we all are the same, we are all created to be connected, and we are all relevant to each other

This book will show you how to deal with the stigma of singleness and the challenge of loneliness. You will discover how to form a healthy and productive relationships, how to redirect sexual desires as a single person, how to resolve conflicts in a more effective way, and how to strengthen the relationships that you have. You too can have and enjoy the best of every relationship.